THE
BE
BOOK

A Journey Into Miracles and
Guide to Self-Liberation

MYNOO MARYEL

The BE Book

A Journey Into Miracles and Guide to Self-Liberation

First published in 2016 by
Panoma Press Ltd
48 St Vincent Drive, St Albans, Herts, AL1 5SJ UK
info@panomapress.com
www.panomapress.com

Cover design by Michael Inns
Artwork by Karen Gladwell

ISBN 978-1-78452-085-4

This book is available online and in all good bookstores.

CONTENTS

Acknowledgements   vii

Introduction   xi

Part ONE: Growing Up   1

CHAPTER 1:   BE Me   3

CHAPTER 2:   BE Fun, BE Fab, BE Fulfilled   13

CHAPTER 3:   BE Wonder Full   19

CHAPTER 4:   BE Free or Be Indifferent   27

CHAPTER 5:   BE Connected   43

Part TWO: Glowing Up   49

CHAPTER 6:   BE Extraordinary   51

CHAPTER 7:   BE Joy   61

CHAPTER 8:   BE Awake   73

CHAPTER 9:   BE Present, BE Real   85

Part THREE: The Big Fat Indian Wedding   93

CHAPTER 10:   BE Trust   95

CHAPTER 11:   BE Love and BE Loved   109

Part FOUR: To BE List or To Do List   117

CHAPTER 12:   Sounds of Heaven   119

CHAPTER 13:   The A-list of the BE List   125

Part FIVE: BE Cause or Be Lost   135

CHAPTER 14:   BE Have or Be Gone   137

CHAPTER 15:   BElong or Be Low   147

CHAPTER 16:   BE Kind or Be Behind   155

Part SIX: BE Live and BEcome   163

CHAPTER 17:   Honey BEs
                    List of BE Words and Their Meanings   165

CHAPTER 18:   BE Tools   169

CHAPTER 19:   BE Stories   185

Part SEVEN: To BE or Not to BE ... What is Your Answer?   201

CHAPTER 20:   Making The BE Move   203

CHAPTER 21:   Readers' Feedback   207

                    Glossary   215

                    About the Author   221

                    Testimonials   223

                    Notes   225

ACKNOWLEDGEMENTS

This book is a co-creation that has come about as a result of my experiences of coming alive, propelled by my soul family and inspired by spirit guides and many metaphysical masters. I would like to acknowledge them all and express my specific gratitude to:

- Several men in my life for the experiences that form the bedrock of the learnings I share here: my father, my ex-husband, my former partner, my twin flame, my maternal grandfather, my mentors and my previous business partners.

- My darling son Sai who, whilst meditating under a special tree in Regent's Park, taught me the gift of listening to my inner wisdom. He continues to inspire, guide and protect me to this day.

- My sister Vibha, who stepped into her magnificent mastery, became the vibe queen and held the vibration high for me to get this work completed within three weeks in Dubai, in the summer of 2015.

- My friend and business partner JP, whose gift of holding the space for my emergence into my true self and being uncompromising in my realizing the mission of my soul has made it possible to convert the received wisdom into this book and many more to follow.

- My niece Surabhi, for being there with me making this work more widely accessible. She completed two other handwritten manuscripts and cards to go with them at the same time as I was creating this work. We inspired each other to keep going and enjoyed each step of the journey.

- Mindy, my book midwife. She got me started on this journey of becoming an author four years ago and in that time I have authored several books. She provided the structure and methodology that helped me to receive the contents of this book during my flight from Denver to Philadelphia in the summer of 2015.

- Lauren, for focusing my attention on the target audience I have the greatest impact on and my unique gift of the BE philosophy. She clarified that the audience for this work is people who are going through a transformational transition where they have to make a choice.

- Martha, whose eye for precision, quality and detail got me to convert my mind maps into the full detailed content of this book. This was key to enabling me to complete it within such a short time.

- Ellen, my intuitive guide, friend and partner in co-creating the experience of bringing heaven on earth.

- Jon, the shamanic high priest, who interrupted the rat race pattern, enabling me to reclaim my destiny through a powerful shamanic ritual.

- Buana and his family, for taking me and my twin flame under their wing, dressing us up in traditional costume and preparing the beautiful offerings that we took to the Balinese temples after dark, when the divine energy vortexes were the strongest.

- The amazing people who are representative of the ideal audience for this work, who agreed to give me their feedback on the first draft of this book. Thank you Amanda, Hindy, Mary, Lija, Sameera, Surabhi, Gaelyn, Daya, Xavier, Ranga, Mindy, Maxime, Adam, Sara, Ruby, Meenal and Tammy.

- My mother, for her dedication to keep us connected to our own spirit and to the teachings of our Hindu scriptures, even when I rejected them in my arrogant phase of ignorance. I remain grateful for her unconditional love and acceptance of my fractured human disguise, always connecting to my brilliance, placing me in my magnificence. Her guidance and teachings continue to flow through me even now, inspiring and supporting my evolution.

Throughout the book, to protect their privacy, I have changed many people's names and personal profiles. I am deeply grateful to you all.

Introduction

The Question

To BE or not to BE... as posed in the opening soliloquy by Prince Hamlet in William Shakespeare's play *Hamlet*... **that is THE question!**

This book is written as an answer to this question. By way of introduction to the book, here is my philosophy in seven key points, which will introduce you to each of the seven parts of the book.

1. It is a choice that we make, to DO or to BE. I choose BEing. My intention is that at some point as you go through this book you too will make an empowered choice and see the rationale in choosing to BE, rather than be caught up in the DO race.

2. We all go through life experiences unique to us. I share here a collection of enchanting journeys in different phases of my life. These journeys formed the pieces of the jigsaw that became a solid, unwavering platform for me: to live my life in such a way that BEing BEcame my state of choice, and doing just flowed flawlessly from there.

3. We each have our story and as you read mine, I invite you to consider your own experiences, especially those that have inspired or impacted you. There is learning in all types of experiences, so open yourself to receive the insights from your own life.

4. I am sharing here my personal journey, my map to
    becoming my own GURU. You can use it as a template and
    apply it to your own terrain. I invite you to examine your
    life and to assess the foundation that was created for you as
    a result.

5. I believe it's time to BECOME the full embodiment of you.
    **BE COME means to BE your own GURU and COME into
    your true inheritance, which is magnificence.** I invite you
    to join me on this magnificent ride.

6. I have come to accept that there are no coincidences or
    synchronicities; everything that occurs in our life – good,
    bad, ugly and beautiful – is by divine design, to support us
    in emerging into our true self. Our choices in these
    moments determine whether we can evolve into the highest
    being we can possibly be, or we continue running in the
    rat race.

7. Finally, we are always choosing even when we choose to
    allow someone else to make the choice for us or during
    those times when we choose to make no choice. I live my
    life with great awareness in the choices I make. I do so with
    the specific intent to come ALIVE in each moment.

The content and layout of each chapter, the incidents and stories
shared were all received on a flight from Denver to Philadelphia in
the summer of 2015. The book, chapters and chapter headings, as well
as the stories and wisdom illustrated through them just flowed with
ease and grace.

I have included them as I received them, trusting and knowing that
the flow and layout of the material —which I believe is simple yet
deep, easy yet able to rattle us out of our comfort zones— will have the
desired impact, creating a new opening for guided, inspired action.

Some of the stories chosen came as a surprise. For me, they were
cute memories from my childhood, which I would not have chosen
to share as an adult. There were others from my adult life that were

deeply personal, somewhat embarrassing and sometimes distressing. Writing this book, sharing what I was guided to share, has made me realize and understand that each little episode that has taken place in my life created its own unique BE foundation, that has enabled me to BE in my essence in each moment.

With great enthusiasm and anticipation I invite you to join me on the ride in the BE state.

The BE Book in 10 minutes or less

This book is written in such a way that each chapter is a complete lesson in itself. If you implement the nuggets from even one of these chapters, and do so consistently, your life will transform beyond your expectations. That is my promise and I make it from my own experience of living this way, moment by moment. Whatever you do, simply **BE in your joy and you will BE in flow.**

I have summarized here the essence of each of the seven parts of the book so that you may get a flavor of its content and flow. It will also enable you to choose which part you wish to dive into more deeply, if you opt to be more creative in your assimilation of these materials.

The first five parts cover the key events and life experiences on my journey of emergence into my true self. These experiences were essential to the birth of the BE in me. The sixth part includes additional support tools, and stories that will serve you well, should you choose to embark on the BE lifestyle yourself.

Part ONE: *Growing Up*

We begin with the backstories that were the seeds for my transcendent life. The first takes place at age two in India, and we wind up at my days as a busy, driven corporate executive in London, where I was experiencing material success while at the same time going deeper and deeper into the dark night of my soul. Zoom with me into different formative experiences, when the rebel in me was born. I take you from my secret explorations of the ancient palaces in India, to my stint in Saudi Arabia, where I found myself gently holding an African dictator as he went through an emotional crisis, to getting drawn into London and catapulted out, 29 years later, right into the lap of my dark night.

Part TWO: *Glowing Up*

This is the story of my emergence into the calling of my soul. A series of powerful (though sometimes frightening) choices connected me to my soul's mission and conceived its manifestation on the planet. This journey was essential for me to become the birth mother of the PoEM, the Palace of Extraordinary Miracles, which is a global template project supporting transformation in relationships. It required me to shed further layers of memories that I held in my cells and within my physical body.

I had to transform even further to enable the project to be birthed. Join me as I travel from London to Bali, from Australia to Mount Shasta and Utah. Follow me through my personal transformations and physical reinventions, as I experience the opening of my third eye, shave my head, meet my twin flame, meet my avatars the dolphins, get support from the kangaroos and unify with St. Germain and the Ascended Masters.

This chapter represents a very different evolution of my life, one that even I did not understand. It was all happening, so I knew the reality of what was going on. After several years of trying to make sense of it all, I chose to let go and allow myself to receive the gifts and the wisdom, to enjoy the after effects and relish the experiences. I invite you too to let go of the need to figure out what is happening. Receive the insights and messages while enjoying the stories being shared.

Part THREE: *The Big Fat Indian Wedding*

You are now invited into the colorful magical choreography of the big fat Indian wedding. My experiences here and beyond were stark naked and deep, completely "in my face" — I was given the nickname "turnip face" at my family's most public function ever, with over 1800 guests in attendance. I received a tremendous gift of humility and connection to true love and romance: I learned to BE Beauty, and beauty emerged from within me. It was a journey of consolidating the lessons from my life in such a way that the BE was born and I was prepared to bring forth the mission of my soul. I share my date with God at the wedding, which led to the unveiling of what it is to be HUMAN. I understood that when **I BE Love, I can BE Loved and I BEcome the BEloved, magnifying and magnetizing my BEloved.**

Part FOUR: *To BE List or To Do List*

I take you with me into "The Zone", where we have a lesson from the Lord of Heaven, Indra, on the BE way of living our lives. I choose to let go of the compulsion to have a "To Do" list. I start to live an intentional life and choose to have a BE list instead. I achieve the results I desire and plan for, faster and with greater precision than I ever did before, and all occurs with so much ease, grace and joy.

I invite you to let go of any confusion that may arise from the metaphysical dimension of my story. It is a part of the process, so read it as you would science fiction, absorbing the lessons as they arise. I share the first seven days in this journey where I am given **the A-list of the BE List.** These are the seven KEY states that make all the difference when you arrive at a pivot point in your life where you *must* make a choice: on one end of that pivot is love and on the other is fear.

Part FIVE: *BE Cause or Be Lost*

This part is about becoming the cause in our matter. We can BE at cause, or we are lost in confusion. Here we really get on a roll in mastering the BE life.

In this section I share my journey into understanding that we are meant to have an easy life. We are meant to have whatever we desire and we are even gifted the words **BE HAVE** as a reminder. **You BE the vibration that matches your desire and you can HAVE what you asked for.**

Unfortunately the two words were conjoined and it became a reprimand instead —"BEHAVE!" — a phrase that has been used to put a stop to unsavory behavior. It is a reprimand that often invites rebelliousness, in direct opposition to the original intent.

I also share my gift from three mountains —Mt. Shasta, Mt. Kailash and Mt. Batur— the gift that instilled the BE experience in every cell of my being. Receive the nuggets of insight and enjoy the vividness of the experiences that led to them.

In **BElong or Be Low** I share my understanding that the times in my life when I felt most depressed and wanted to hide were fueled by the fear that I did not belong. Here I share my inspiration to rise from below and belong.

BE Kind or Be Behind: This chapter is all about being kind to yourself —your physical, emotional, mental, ethereal and spiritual self— otherwise, you deplete yourself of life force and joy and you do get left behind. I reveal the message I received from Amma, India's hugging saint, the essence of which is that, "You *are* your mother. You birth yourself every single day...so what if you were to treat yourself with the unconditional love and acceptance you would give to your newborn?" Implementing this advice has transformed my life and that of many others with whom I have shared this.

We end with the **evolution from I AM (my self-identity) to BE AM (beaming the light of being in my truth)**, becoming at one with my higher self and stepping into the realm of super coherence.

Part SIX: *BE Live and BEcome*

This part is about bringing the learnings in this book alive and supporting you in becoming true to yourself.

Here I include the **HONEY BEs, the nectar of 27 BE words** for you to choose from. If you like, you may choose a different one each day. Give it your own meaning (or borrow mine) and step into your dancing shoes, dancing and living to the rhythms of your soul.

There is a chapter with BE Tools that support you in getting on track or returning to the BE state if you happen to have fallen off track. These are tools that lift your vibration and keep you in the moment. There is also a set of three specific meditations that both beginners and advanced meditators can put into practice.

We finish with four BE Stories of people in situations that had caught them in the busy-ness trap of doing. Step-by-step, I share their journey of transformation.

Part SEVEN: *To BE or Not to BE... What is Your Answer?*

This is my invitation to you to make the BE move.

I share how some readers are using this work as well as feedback from others in different phases of transition who agreed to review and apply this work in their own lives.

We end with a glossary of some of the less common words used in the book.

One final note: having lived in India and England, and having travelled extensively across the world, I seem to have developed my own unique style of communicating in English. Please do tune into it to make it work for you.

PART ONE:

GROWING UP

During a flight from Denver to Philadelphia I was given the entire structure for this book, including the chapters, the sections and the subsections. I was also shown specific episodes from my life that established the foundation of the BE rather than the DO way of living my life. This was my secret to coming alive and being optimistic in any situation, no matter what cards I felt I had been dealt.

The collection of stories in this section is what I was guided to include. I then verified them by speaking with people who are still around and were present during my early childhood. So, just in case you wonder how I am able to remember in such precise detail situations that took place when I was two or three or five years old, know that I did so with some assistance.

I was surprised to find the correlations, in each episode, to who I have become and what I am bringing about as I follow the mission of my soul. I am grateful for the early foundation that was established in this way. The experience of narrating these stories in this book has been a gift, reinforcing my knowing that we are always cared for and looked after by forces beyond our human comprehension.

CHAPTER 1

BE ME

Finding Ma

This story goes back to when I was just over two years old. I was brought up by my aunt and grandparents, as my mom was doing her PhD in a different town and my dad was busy settling into his new job as a bank officer. My grandma ran a school. I was taken to school every morning and loved being the center of attention, though my joyful experiences were often interrupted by somber interludes, when I would be quite on my own and did not speak with anyone. No one knew why I had these interrupts, until one day I decided to run away from the school, toddling my way out on to the main street.

My grandparents were very well known in the town and the school was very popular. In those days school pick-up was by rickshaw, and one day the rickshaw rider saw little Mynoo toddling away down the road. He came over to me and asked me where I was going. I said, "I am going to see my Ma." He realized that I had run away from school and, not realizing my ma was studying in a different town, he said he would take me to her. So I jumped onto his rickshaw and off we went. I had a big beaming smile on my face, so excited was I to meet my mother.

After riding in the rickshaw for several minutes, he brought me to a large house. We got down and I ran into the gates of the house, only to find my grandfather, grandmother, aunt and several other people from the neighborhood. They were all showing love and concerned excitement to see me; they were gushing away, showering me with accolades and presents, telling me what a good girl I was and that they loved me.

Despite the crowd, I felt alone. Where was Ma? I felt betrayed and deeply disappointed; like I had been taken for a ride, misled and controlled. I recall these feelings clearly, though I only know the story because it has been narrated to me so many times. This is my first memory of making the choice to **BE Independent, so I can rely on myself.** I made the decision to keep this a secret and pretend that all was well. For my family, they realized for the first time that even though the love I was receiving was huge and the care immaculate, I still missed my Ma and no one could replace her. They finally understood my somber interludes and realized they had to do something about it. And guess what? I got more time with Ma! I understood that **it pays off to BE Me** and to express what I want, while still being independent enough that no one could control me or push me around. The rebel in me was born.

No Gift for Me?

When I was three years old, my sister was born. I was very excited to have her and loved playing with this little baby. She was so cute, with lots of curly hair like Lord Krishna and many people commented on that. I was happy being special because she was so precious. I felt the happy responsibility as big sister and enjoyed showing her off to friends and protecting her from too much attention, keeping her safe in her baby cot.

A few months after her birth, there was a special ceremony to welcome her and officially name her. The house was splendid, with colorful displays, the aromas of yummy foods and the excited anticipation of all the guests who were to arrive bearing gifts. I always loved such functions and gatherings and this time I had my little sister to show and share with all my uncles and aunts.

They all arrived with gifts for the newborn. I was happy, so happy until the evening when, just as I was falling asleep, I realized that nobody had given me any gifts. So I decided to ask my favorite aunt about this in the morning. I woke up early, excited to start another day with my cute sis and hoping to share the gifts I received with her. The festivities and entertainment going on during the day carried us all away.

In the evening, my favorite aunt stayed with me until I fell asleep. I remembered to ask her about my gifts. So, as I lay on her lap, I asked in my sweet little voice, "Bua (Aunty), will no one bring any gifts for me anymore?" She was surprised and touched by the innocence of my question and cuddled me lovingly, saying, "It's not like that; you are now the older sister and we will take you to the shops to choose your own gifts." I was happy and satisfied by this response and fell asleep in her arms. She then laid me on my bed and left the room to join the rest of the family and visiting guests, who were all sitting out in the courtyard getting ready for dinner.

I woke up again and stood by the window behind the drapes, feeling excited, not wanting to miss out on the fun the adults were having.

I overheard Mom ask my aunt if I had gone to sleep, as I had seemed very energized.

She replied, "Yes, she did, and before she slept she asked me so sweetly, 'Will no one buy me any gifts?'"

"Aww..." was the sigh from the guests, and a few of them laughed.

Ma asked, "What did you say?"

Auntie replied, "I told her she is now a big girl, we will take her shopping and she can choose her own gifts." Everyone laughed, and then moved on to the next conversation.

I started crying. I knew no one was watching and this time I sobbed quietly, covering my mouth with my little hands, stopping myself from making any sounds. I did not want anyone to hear or see me crying. I made another key decision that night: **BE Strong,** do not share how you feel with anyone; they will just laugh at you. How you feel is your secret, it's not for anyone to know.

This was the beginning of the slow shut-down of my connection to my heart. My desires, visions and plans became my secret companions. I became a smiling, playful yet aloof child, with lots to share and talk about with people, but I never shared about myself or what I desired for myself. I became known for being strong, very accommodating, while also being a leader in any crowd.

BEing Swept Off My Feet

My grandfather was an accomplished Ayurvedic doctor and also the head of several villages. My grandparents lived in the town where Lord Krishna had been born, called Mathura. My grandfather was a generous leader of his people, so the villagers would come to see him with their ailments and he would treat them, pro bono, with Ayurvedic protocols and medications. He would also feed them and give them a place to stay if they had traveled from far away. As a result, when he held his clinics there were many, many people who showed up for treatment.

For the first three years of my life my grandparents raised me, and until the age of five I still spent a lot of time with them. When I was staying there, what I loved most was being with Nana (Grandpa) when he held his clinics. I would sit on this little footstool next to him and he would talk me through his diagnosis, using a three-dimensional wooden cut-out of the human body, which was at least as tall as I was.

I found it extremely interesting to be so involved and engaged in this work. I also had the joy of feeling blessed when patients who had been cured came by to express their gratitude. I was the one they tapped on the head to bless for the grace showered on them by God and my grandfather. When the cured patients brought gifts, they always had something special for me, too. It felt like important work and I loved being a part of it.

Everything was conducted in the open, and only in exceptional circumstances would Nana go into a private room to examine a patient. His clinic was like a town hall gathering, with a great sense of community spirit and connection. Everyone could hear and even share their opinions about the ailments with which people presented themselves. Nana was very focused and so was I, when I was with him, doing what was necessary for the patient to get well. For me, too, going to the clinic was like going to do some important work each day.

On one of the clinic days, we were deep into the queue of patients when an old man arrived with his son. The old man was groaning and in severe pain. We had not seen them before. Nana asked a number of diagnostic questions, felt his pulse, looked at his tongue and was just starting to examine his tonsils and his eyes. He was explaining to me with the body image what he was doing and what he had found. I was deeply engrossed in the diagnosis with him.

I was just getting up to stand on my stool to be able to get closer to the patient's throat and eyes as they were being examined, when I was whisked off my feet and taken away, perched on the shoulder of the old man's son. I was in complete shock: angry, very, very upset and screaming to be set down again. I recall kicking my little legs and trying to free my hands, which were held so tightly by the old man's son. He was trying to keep me away from the scene below. I could see my grandfather was treating the old man's eyes with some drops. My own eyes were welling up with tears and I finally bit the man who was holding me away from doing what I loved. He set me down on the ground and I ran out of the clinic and into my room, where I cried my heart out.

I made another decision then, that I could not become too engrossed in doing what I loved most. Instead, I had to **BE Vigilant** at all times, so that no one could sweep me off my feet; because when that happens, they control me and I have to fight my way out of the situation; I lose what I love and am left to cry alone. I also chose to never share what I truly LOVED with anyone, just in case they might decide to sweep me off my feet and take me away. From then on, my acute observations of people and the goings-on around me, all of my enchanting adventures and surprising experiences, became my own secret world. It was a world where I loved to be, but where no one else was allowed.

I recently found out that the old man had had a severely infectious condition; his son was simply keeping me away from it.

Defining Choice

At the age of five I decided that I was going to be a world-famous heart surgeon, in particular, the one who was going to invent the cure for all heart disease. I openly shared with people that I was going to be a heart surgeon, but kept my vision of becoming world-renowned for my inventions as my secret. I started training myself in my own way to achieve this.

Here are two of the strange ways I chose to train, cultivating my ability to do anything in any situation.

Earliest Lesson in BEing

Every year before we went to visit my grandparents, I would ask my mother to train me to narrate a story from the stage, for a gathering of hundreds of students and adults. We would choose the story for its strong moral lessons and by the time we went on our visit, I was prepared to perform in front of a live audience. Nana would take me to the villages where he was the chief and a gathering of all the schools would be called.

A big table was placed on the stage and I stood on it, with a microphone almost as large as my head in front of me. I would narrate the story in English, and with great pride and joy share the moral of the story. The audience did not understand a word I was saying as they all spoke Braj Bhasha, but the energy of how I performed was infectious. I was clearly loving every minute of sharing the story. I had practiced it so often that it felt completely natural when I spoke it on the stage. I filled my narration with expression and ended with a crescendo, leaving the audience on a high, pondering what the moral of the story might be.

The audience was riveted; children were excitedly clapping and jumping at the end, and the adult teachers had tears streaming down their faces. Nana, with moistened eyes himself, looked at me so proudly, and, as a reward, I was allowed to go running through the fields with my friend, a young lad who was very protective of me. I loved slushing through the sugar cane fields. My very favorites, though, were the fields of green gram (chickpeas). I have such fond memories of plucking the little green grams, peeling them with my little fingers and eating the sweet seed within. We would chase the butterflies and pretend to be scarecrows, waving a brightly-colored scarf around to keep the sparrows away.

We would visit the cowherd and he would milk the cow right in front of us. Then we would drink a little fresh raw milk in a kuladh (a cup made of mud). I fondly remember the scent of moistened mud mixed with the milk. The last stop before I returned to join Nana was a visit to the women by the village well. They would pull the water out of the well and pour it on my feet to wash them, singing folk songs as they were doing this. If Nana was still busy, I would be sent off to be with the head of the village's family. I remember watching in fascination as the men and women gathered there to weave their own cotton and raw silk, a practice they had adopted during the freedom struggle and which continues to this day. I also watched with curiosity as two bulls went round and round in a circle, extracting mustard oil (I was never allowed in the room, all I could see were two bulls walking around in a circle).

These experiences were my earliest lessons in BEing. I spoke in English and Hindi, the villagers in Braj Bhasha. **I chose to BE Enchanted.** It was the vibration of my being that engaged with and enthralled the audience and the villagers. They were true to their nature in doing what each was best at. I felt that, and I knew I was safe even when my grandfather was busy with his village governance meetings. I experienced the joy of mixing song, dance, food and frolic with serious work, and seeing people doing all of this collaboratively, so the jobs got done. I chose the stories for their moral conclusions and this was habit-forming. I realize now that starting from that very tender age I have frequently spent time in solitude, pondering and distilling the morals and lessons of my life experiences up to that moment in time.

Try it for yourself: At the end of each day, take a few moments to just be with yourself; ask yourself what you have learned from all your experiences that day. Managed solitude is a weekly practice for me and one I adopted at an early age.

Walking on the Ceiling

My mother had grown up in a family of freedom fighters. Half of her family had been revolutionaries and followers of Subhash Chandra Bose, and the other half had followed Gandhi and his nonviolence movement. For many, many years until I left home, Ma shared stories of courage and strategy, starring not just leaders such as Gandhi, Jesus and the many amazing figures from Indian mythology, she also shared the real-life experiences of people from her own family and friends who had led the freedom movement in India.

She awakened the curiosity in me to always BE Learning; the knowing that it is never too late and the reassurance that I never had to feel too shy to ask for inspiration. She planted the seed in me to seek inspiration in everyday happenings, as well as in role models and the iconic events that shape the course of history.

When I was six years old, we had chores to do at home and my job was to set the dining table every evening. We always ate dinner together as a family.

We ate from thalis (large stainless steel plates). I would take the plates and walk from the kitchen to the dining room, gazing into the reflection of the ceiling on the plate. It was initially frightening to find myself walking on the ceiling; then, as I practiced, I became a master at it. I could even run on the ceiling reflected on my plate. This, in my view, was a major achievement.

One day as I was gloating and rather pleased with myself for having made that first run while looking at the reflection, Ma came into the dining room and asked me what I was doing. I told her and she became angry at me for having risked my safety; I could have fallen and hurt myself badly, over a silly act! That's when I shared my secret with her. "Ma, you know what? I am going to be world-famous for my invention that will cure all forms of heart disease. I have to be prepared for this, so I am learning to do challenging things that others would not attempt and now I have conquered my fear of the unknown."

At six I already knew I could do whatever it took, as long as I can BE Courageous and BE Knowing that I will succeed.

My mother hugged me, told me I was cute and promised to guide me by sharing the stories of world leaders who made the impossible happen, so that I could learn from them. How blessed I was!

What inspires you, and how does it shape your choices?

CHAPTER 2:

BE FUN, BE FAB, BE FULFILLED

My World Order

I started defining my world order as I entered primary school and saw myself as a popular yet assertive queen of the realm that I was living in. I realize now that I was starting to co-create my destiny by imagining new worlds into being and enjoying every moment of my existence in that reality. Then I was pulled back into the reality of school, grades and competing with my dearest friends because the systems demanded it, while at the same time being super helpful and supportive to those students who were lagging behind.

I chose to work with Ma and the teachers at school to get the top grades, so that my dad did not need to get involved in my schooling. He had far less patience than my mother or teachers. I was determined to establish my position as a leader so I could not be pushed around on account of academics. Academic achievement was important in our home and I was good at it.

I created my own structure and played it like a game. I became a master at it, to such an extent that I could achieve the grades that impressed while at the same time excelling at extracurricular activities such as dance, painting, sewing, cooking – the sorts of things Indian girls are taught so they can become eligible brides. I soon became a teacher's pet and the one most parents compared their kids to. Suffice it to say that my circle of friends started to diminish. I, however, was on such a roll that I didn't care about that.

I was going to get through to high school with grades and all, looking pretty and having all it takes to make the perfect Indian bride. I was not going to marry yet, though. I just wanted to know that I had the best choices should I choose to go in that direction. I became so good at what I did that I was invited to represent my state in a group of hand-picked students who were chosen by the Homi Baba Nuclear Institute to co-lead nuclear power research projects. I was the youngest in the group and the only one from a school; the others were all college degree students. I was often asked by my teachers at school to become the teacher for the day. The three subjects I was the worst at – math, chemistry and physics – became my favorite ones.

I also got a double promotion in school, so I was moved from kindergarten directly into second grade and then again from second to fourth grade. I was the youngest and the smallest in my class, too. I knew I had to work very hard to comprehend and catch up with the knowledge being taught in the class. I was privileged to have all the added support from the teachers and my mom. Dad tried hard and patiently to teach me math and finally gave up, his patience ran out. I learned a big lesson through this experience.

For my dad, I was not good at math and physics, and so I was not. According to him I needed to be controlled as well as directed, so I would easily get distracted when studying with him. I was BEing exactly as he expected me to BE. I found myself constantly rebelling against my dad. It was my way of exercising my independence: BE Strong, BE Independent, BE Rebellious. I felt my rebelliousness was totally justified, though in hindsight I can see it must have made it hard for Mom and Dad. It only made my father want to control me even more. The cycle continued. My rebelliousness led me to become adventurous and the experiences that resulted were formative to say the least. The gift of excessive control by my father led me to becoming a clever strategist, where I could enjoy being a free spirit while at the same time conforming to the expected norms. I had found the winning formula and I was living it.

For my mother and my teachers, I was this super-bright, all-rounder child who was making their school proud, and so I was. According to them, I was self-motivated, directed and determined. As a result, I became focused and achieved the desired results, while being a great dancer, good housekeeper, artist, seamstress and cook, all at the same time. I also loved sports and was good at badminton as well as basketball. With my mother and teachers and as a result of them, I was being free, certain and self-confident.

In going over this phase of my life again, in retrospect I can see that my games at being a teacher or a leader with my tribe of friends, soft toys and cushions were times where I was teaching myself while pretending to be educating them. I did so in a fun way, applying my imagination and enjoying BEing the leader I was to become.

I also see that my structured system, the one that guaranteed my grades in school, is the one I draw on when I am working on urgent, high-priority tasks, even today. I used the same system with my son, preparing him for his 11 plus, GCSE and A-level exams in England several years later. It's a system of dividing the day into 40-minute work/study slots, each followed by a 20-minute break/play slot. I also had time set aside for lunch and play (an hour each). I started my day at 7:00 am and finished at 10:30 pm or earlier. I did this for at least two weeks and sometimes three weeks prior to exams. I was full of energy, balanced with certainty and confidence, knowing I was prepared and ready for the challenge before me, while many of my peers were nervous, anxious and sleep-deprived.

Everyone is a Leader

This is a specific experience that collapsed my two realities: the world I was imagining into being and the one that we were in – the rat race. I was eight years old, and I always saw myself as the leader of a clan. My clan was often represented by my friends, my soft toys and cushions. My leadership style was education-based, and I would go to great lengths to teach about new discoveries and facilitate exploration, adventures and discussions about what I was uncovering.

One such evening, I was with my toys and soft cushions, teaching about leadership and how they could each live a happier life (from my perspective as an eight-year-old who had it all figured out!). I was talking, dancing around, singing and clapping. This went on for hours. I felt the buzz, I enjoyed the beauty I was surrounded with, knowing that I could do whatever I wanted, because not only was I the leader, but each person in my class was a part of a special force and was a leader in their own right.

I was allocating jobs and sharing ways of achieving greater efficiency, solving problems, when the door opened and in walked my father. He asked me assertively what I was doing there and before I could answer, he said that that was enough of me trying to avoid doing my homework. This was not the case, as I had already completed my homework, but Dad would have none of this and I was put into a room in the house and locked in. The only set of keys was left with Ma.

I felt shocked and crushed. I made a conscious choice to snap out of the drama and **BE the leader** who leads and does not allow emotional upheaval to get in the way — a leader whose only job is to create other leaders who can also take failure and not give a damn. "I have a big job to do," I told myself. "I cannot let the weakness of bullies or the hurt from my father stop me." I understood then that if I reacted by showing aggression back at my dad or with my sister, I would become a bully myself. That would make me weak, and I had already made the choice to BE Strong.

Fun and Fab

I went through a phase in my life as a little girl where I became an unstoppable rebel and my dad resorted to his favorite punishment of locking me up in a room for several hours at a time, depending on the naughtiness I had indulged in. I figured out a way to squeeze my flexible little body out of the window and sneak out to play with our servants' kids. My father was a bank officer and we lived in the officers' colony. Our apartment was on the ground floor.

I recall having the most fabulous time with these kids, my Tamil (south Indian language) improved rapidly and the servants' kids started using Hindi and English words. We would go climbing trees, hanging from the branches, plucking tamarind and wood apple. We chucked this hard fruit from the top of the tree to the ground to break it open, and excitedly climbed down to share it together. I would return to the room I had been locked into just in time, looking suitably guilty for my mom when she opened the door to let me out. This was my secret world and fortunately, no one squealed.

I would spend some time being hugged and cuddled by Mom, who was feeling guilty for having followed Dad's instructions, and was extra supportive with my homework assignments. She would then dress me up so I would look fabulous when I went out to play with the children of my parents' friends. This is the time I call my fab time. We would put on plays and dance shows of *Snow White* and *Cinderella* for our parents. It was very civilized and sweet.

All was perfect until one day I overstepped the mark so far that Dad became extremely upset. This time, his instructions were to lock me in the room and to keep me there until he returned from work. I was to have no food that day, because I had been extremely greedy and upset my little sister by taking her share of the pastries. I was absolutely thrilled, as this time I could go with my fun friends, the servants' kids, to their fishing village on the beach and go fishing using the nets in the ocean. I did not have to return until the evening!

So off we went, for the most thrilling fun I had ever had as a kid, riding on the back of a rickety old scooter. All five of us kids piled up on each other. We got to the fisherman's shack on the beach and went out into the ocean to fish. It was only a short sail into the ocean, so we did not catch anything, but it was exciting. So much fun! I returned to the room that I had been locked into well in time, so I would have some time to rest before Dad returned home. To my surprise, as I jumped into the room from the window, I found the door open and heard the voices of my father and other adults, very animated and agitated.

I realized then that my mom must have come into the room at lunchtime (of course she was not going to let her little Mynoo go hungry), found that I was not there, hailed security, called dad and a search party was set up. Then I returned and was caught in the act, red-handed. I was in real trouble then and the locking me into the room stopped. My rebelliousness subsided, too. I had hurt my mom, my dad, my sister and myself and it was just enough.

I learned that I could continue to BE Fun in my circle of fabulous friends, so the thrill of having fun returned. I also learned that social class segregation was unnecessary and deep down we are the same if we choose to think that way. I was just as well cared for by the servants, looked after in a delicate way and accepted with open arms with no expectations; they just shared their joy with me. This experience took away the judgment and evaluation that plagues many relationships. Keeping up with the Joneses was an attitude that I could not relate to, not ever, because I saw first-hand that the servants in their homes had everything that made them feel fulfilled, while many of my mom and dad's wealthy friends did not notice what they had and continued to feel deprived.

I got the power of **BE Fun and you have the fun you want. BE Fab and you feel fabulous. BE Fulfilled and you enjoy whatever you have wherever you are.**

Try it for yourself and enjoy the difference.

CHAPTER 3:

BE WONDER FULL

Fields of Melons

We spent our summer vacations visiting family and my grandparents in the north of India, where I developed this unusual fascination with finding and exploring underground passages in old palaces.

All over India there were many old palaces and they often had elaborate escape routes, so that the royals, along with their entourages, could escape when enemies took the palace over in battle. It was especially exciting for me, because even though we entered the underground passage from within the palace grounds, we did not know where it would lead. In my childhood naïvete, I just *knew* that we would come out somewhere exotic and surprising. It was a thrilling adventure that I completely enjoyed, another secret game that had to be undertaken without the adults knowing, as they would be boring and impose their fears and restrictions on us.

I have enjoyed many such exploratory adventures, some of them quite creepy and scary because of the skulls and bones we found along the way. Each and every time, though, we came out safe and emerged somewhere just wonderful, into the arms of the warm sunshine. This was my very favorite feeling, as it could get quite cold and damp down under the palaces.

There are two adventures I am guided to share here for the foundational impact they have had in shaping my thinking and personality.

I had relatives who lived in an ancient palace on the banks of the river Yamuna in Vrindavan, the town where Lord Krishna was brought up when he was a baby. It was a quaint, very religious town filled with hundreds of Hindu temples. I was 11 years old that summer. I gathered my little cousins and their friends and we decided to go exploring to find the underground passage. I had already become quite the expert at finding the entrance to such escape routes, and this one was easy.

Three of the kids accompanied me as we went in to explore. This entrance was more like a cave, larger than usual. It had stacks of hay piled up in front of it and long thick rope-like leashes attached, as if the local donkey herder were using it for his donkeys. We climbed up, then crawled through and on top of the hay, to get to a place that was familiar territory to me. This was an escape route all right, and a much-travelled one too. The walls were dry and the floor less slushy than many others I had travelled through.

We started walking. And walking. And walking, until the light disappeared and it was dark. We had to tear apart some spider webs along the way; at least that's what we assumed they were, as we could not see a thing! When you get into this position of complete darkness in an underground escape route, all you can do is to keep walking forward until you see a glimmer of light. The passage felt quite long and the walls seemed to be dripping some kind of liquid.

One of the three kids started crying and insisted on turning back. Her elder sister screamed and told me off, threatening to tell our parents what I had done and where I was taking them. I kept calm, though on the inside, I too was concerned. This passage felt longer than the ones I had explored before. I said with confidence, "I can lead you out of this place but I don't know how to turn back." I kept telling my heart to feel the heat and take us to the sunshine.

I started sharing stories of Lord Krishna's naughtiness and his cute teasing of the ladies of the village we were in. I invited us to explore in our imaginations whether he had ever been where we were. And just then, I saw it: the light. We ran towards it. The opening was small, blocked by a stream of muddy water. We were still able to wade through that and climb out.

The first little girl to emerge was nine and, just as she stepped out, she shrieked with joyous excitement. The second child followed and screamed too, and they both started talking quickly and excitedly. I was so curious: what did they find? Where were we? Every minute felt long and then I was finally out too, in the sunshine in a large field of absolutely huge watermelons.

We ran amok and jumped on the melons. It was naughty, yes, but we didn't care. We were so thrilled to be out and the experience of a watermelon bursting open was just beyond anything we had imagined. We heard a loud angry noise and saw a man with a whip and a flag running towards us, shouting at us to stop what we were doing at once. We all felt like we had conquered the world and just kept going, running, jumping and even rolling in the mud amongst the plants. When I sat up from my roll, I realized that we had crossed the entire river and that the palace was now on the other side.

The angry farmer arrived and simply could not figure out where we had come from, landing right in the middle of his farm. The heat of our excitement had subsided and now we had to find our way home. We told him that we lived in the palace across the river. His wife and his daughter joined in the conversation, also curious about just how we got there. The three of us all spoke at once in such excited voices that they could not understand what we were saying and, before we had a chance to explain any further, we saw that a boat was passing by. The farmer helped us onto the boat and we got home safely.

We rushed into the outside bathrooms and cleaned up before we entered the house. I looked flushed, and had an uncontrollable smile, the widest smile I have ever had on my face. It was an experience that I shared only when I returned to Bombay and wrote an essay on what I did during my summer vacation.

This experience had me embrace **BE the Leader. BE Knowing. BE Trusting that all is well and that we are always taken care of perfectly.** And, once you start the journey, keep going. Just **BE Playful** and the surprises will surprise you. If you stop part of the way there and then turn back, it's a painful, disappointing journey to nowhere. I learned to **BE Magical, immersed in the magic and wonder of life; it's infectious,** it conquers all fear and even turns fearful or angry people into happy supporters.

*Do you remember when you first connected to
the wonder of life? What effect did it have?*

Lucknow to Lemuria

This episode took place when I was nearly 15. I had almost forgotten about it until 2012 when I was in Perth, Australia and visiting a new friend, a woman with whom I had been guided to stay. We were having tea at her home, where I was planning to rent a room. I noticed a framed photograph on the wall with the caption, "The Lucknow Battalion." My friend told me that her son was in this battalion. I replied that I had come from a town close to Lucknow. I wondered why I was being shown this picture.

I knew that there must be some inspiration or connection I was to make, which is why my spirit guides had asked me to stay with her. Prior to our meeting, I had only met her once, at a party. She too was from London and we got along very well. Following my inner guidance, I had emailed her with some hesitation, saying that I was guided to reach out to her and asking her whether it made sense for me to stay at her place. After consulting with her husband she came back with a welcoming email, and now here I was, at her home, looking at The Lucknow Battalion. The plot thickened; I knew this was not the last of it. Perhaps the photo was a reminder of something I was to connect with in Lucknow, where several of my uncles, aunts and cousins lived to this day. With this thought in my mind, I took my leave. We'd agreed that I'd bring my bags over the next day.

That night, as I was reminiscing about Lucknow, I recalled the last time I had been there. As a girl of 14 I and my adventure buddy (a cousin) decided to change our planned itinerary at the last minute, and went to visit our family in Lucknow. It was my first visit there. We were excited because there were many ancient manor homes and palaces from the Mughal times that we were keen to explore.

Our aunt and uncle specifically told us not to go into the maze in one of the palaces, the Bhool Bhulaiyaa in the Bada Imambada. It was an escape route for the Nawabs and their servers. It had been built so that the enemies who followed the escaping rulers would get stuck and confused and not know how to get out of the maze.

The Bhool Bhulaiyaa was made of marble and used mirrors and semi-precious stones to cause a series of reflection and refraction phenomena, so that if you didn't already know your way around, you would not be able to get out of the maze. There were stories of it being haunted, as many people had died there trying to find their way out. There had once been guides to take guests through the maze, but when we were there, it had become derelict and there was no more business for the guides, so they had disappeared, having taken other jobs in the city.

This was a perfect adventure ground for us, so of course we rented two bikes and went. It was very run down. The marble was corroded, though the mirrors were still visible. My cousin and I agreed to explore it all, so we split up as we entered the maze. We were clear that all this stuff about being stuck in there was just the usual adult fears. We knew that we were going to **BE Fine.**

It was exciting and we started our walk. We walked and walked and walked. We turned around and kept walking, and kept returning to the same place. After the fourth time, I stopped. We could hear each other, and we knew we were close from the proximity of our voices, but we could not figure out how to meet and get out of there. Neither of us wanted to go over the conversation from that morning; we just kept our faith that we would be shown.

I started to feel a little tired and thirsty, and responsible for my cousin. Though he was strong, he was still younger than me, and I should have known better than to endanger us both like this. I released this fleeting guilt trip and asked, with complete sincerity, "Please, please, *please* let us find a guide who can take us out". And within minutes a long, tall man, wearing a brocade *sherwani* arrived, and held his hand out to me. I took it, and he walked me out. On the way we met with my cousin and exited the maze together. We were out! We were so happy to see the sky and the grass that we ran around like excited little kids. It was then that I realized that the guide was gone. At the time, I guessed that he'd just had another job to do.

Now, fast forward to 2012. I was getting ready to sleep at my new friend's place. I decided to move the direction of the bed and cover the dysfunctional fireplace; it was drafty on that wintry night and quite cold. As I moved the bed, I heard a thud, and a book fell to the floor. The book was called *Lemuria.* Since my visit to Mount Shasta on 11/11/11, Lemuria had become very interesting to me. I picked up the book and was excited to read it. I switched on my bedside lamp and opened it up. It described the lives and living habits of Lemurians before the great Atlantean-Lemurian battle took place.

And there it was, the Lucknow surprise. Right there in the book was a photo of the guide that had come to safely escort us out of the maze when I was 14. I knew that my cousin had not seen him and thought that I had just found my way out myself. I did not make much of it at the time, as I was spooked myself and didn't want to talk about it.

Having made a powerful connection to Lemuria on Mount Shasta (as well as in Bali, story to follow), I was now ready to make the connection to one of my dear guardian angels, Anton, a master healer from Lemuria. He has been seen on Mount Shasta many times, by people who choose to visit or camp at the mountain. On that occasion in Lucknow, when I was just turning 15, he visited me and guided me to safety at my request; in 2012 he introduced himself to me through his photograph in this Rosicrucian book called *Lemuria*.

This journey from Lucknow to Lemuria left me with a clear message: **BE Safe and you are; BE Accepting and you receive; BE Blessed and be in bliss.**

I knew then beyond the shadow of a doubt that I was, I am and I always will be looked-after, cared for and protected wherever I am, and so it is. I also understood that there are no accidents or synchronicities, only magical happenings, which get us back on track to realizing the missions of our souls.

Have you ever encountered these kinds of parallels, experiences from your childhood that link to happenings in your adult life? Often when this occurs there is a powerful life lesson; can you uncover what that might be for you?

CHAPTER 4:

BE FREE OR
BE INDIFFERENT

We now enter the teenage years and beyond. This was my time in the dragons' den when life presented me with opportunities and an obstacle course that changed from trajectory to trajectory. I had to pitch my ideas and ways to what initially appeared to be a hostile audience, which later became my raving supporters. I know now that these experiences were essential for the solid grounding I had in BEing optimistic. My belief that "this too shall pass" solidified and I resolved that nothing could ever hold me down or push me back. I will survive and even thrive, as long as I keep moving forward.

In Love at 15: *From the Frying Pan into the Fire*

At 15, I fell in love with a handsome, enterprising 19-year-old. He was a complete contrast to me, a polar opposite, which in fact made the relationship exciting and in a strange way quite fulfilling at the time. I was an accomplished academic and had grown up in a stable household where a corporate or bank job was the next logical step. He, on the other hand, had struggled with academics and had barely made it through with passing grades. He was a serial entrepreneur, and was already earning good money through little jobs he had taken with market research companies. My family was full of doctors, PhDs and engineers. His family had a business background; some of them had been very successful and others not so.

We were from different parts of India. I had been born and raised in India in a highly patriotic environment. Beyond that, my grandparents had been active freedom fighters and many of my relatives had lost their lives in the battles to get the British to quit India. My bedtime stories had been about the patriots from my own family. I was Indian and proud to be so. He, on the other hand, had been born in Tanzania. He had a British passport and was waiting for his British residency. His family had put all their hopes on this residency and could not wait to get out of India. While I was an eternal optimist, he was a "glass half empty" person, though desperately keen to learn positive thinking. (Ironically, he was the one who introduced me to books on personal growth and transformation.) It was an unlikely alliance, to say the least.

My father did not approve of the relationship, so that made it all the more attractive to me. I loved his financial independence and it fueled our love affair. I learned about a new culture and also about British etiquette, as he and his family prepared for living in England.

He was quite extreme in how he related to me. On the one hand he had a foul temper, and on the other, he had an intense, loving connection to me. He was strong and determined to become a self-made man and take me to England, where we were to build our "nest". His vision of our life in England was so visually real that I decided to support him to get over his pent-up anger and enjoy life a bit more than he had done until that point.

On the quest of building our "nest," he took a job in Saudi Arabia and I accepted a position straight after my graduation. Instead of following the family tradition and doing my Masters in genetic engineering, I joined a computer consultancy corporation. I was one of just three students chosen from India to do the Masters in the USA. It felt just too stifling, though, so I went against the grain and was employed in a high-flying job that my family did not quite understand. I was being paid more than senior officers in the bank my father worked for. My parents were gracious enough to support me in following my heart and exploring this job that I had chosen. As we were in the very early days of computing in India, I had the opportunity to be trained thoroughly and very professionally by one of the leading computer consultancies there. A foundation of professionalism was created within me, and I went on in later life to become a sought-after project manager and CIO.

We settled into our jobs and were married; I stepped from the frying pan into the fire. We then moved to live in Saudi Arabia and the drama began.

Saudi Arabia
Gourmet Club, Book Club

Within the first week of our being in Saudi Arabia together, one evening my loving husband hit me. It was the first time, but would not be the last. I cried. He said, "This is why I hit you: so you can express your emotions." I was completely taken aback, and my temple of love came crashing down. I felt I had to protect myself while keeping the marriage going.

I decided that I had to find a way to work in Saudi Arabia. I had moved from having a well-established professional standing in India, to looking forward to being a housewife, taking care of my husband and enjoying being in leisure, while creating a beautiful, loving life for us both. Now that he had moved from just being occasionally angry to actually hitting me, I had to return to my choice from earlier in life: **BE Independent, BE Vigilant and BE Free.** Going back was not an option. I felt I had to find another way to remain married, to minimize the damage to myself and to be able to turn him around in a loving and supportive way. This next phase would be about enriching both my career and my marriage.

So the decision was made, and even the strict rules of women not being allowed to work in Saudi did not hold me back. I BEcame certain that a solution would be found, and it was.

The Sheikh of my husband's business had recently married the love of his life, an educated Arabic lady, and he became enthusiastic about his wife and I working together to form an Institute for Computer Studies for Women. I was given a big empty building and carte blanche to do what was necessary to make the Institute happen.

That's when the scale of the task dawned on me. How was I to recruit teachers or students who would be adult Saudi women? This was a challenge because given the rules about women and work, I could not advertise. It had to be an under-the-radar, word-of-mouth approach.

So we formed a Gourmet Club, and we invited one woman from each embassy to be nominated to join the club. We expected that this would be where I would recruit my teachers. A Book Club was also created, for Saudi women who were fluent in English and educated in the west. This is where the students would come from. The strategy delivered perfectly. The Institute was launched and became oversubscribed within three months.

I saw that once I made the decision to thrive, not just survive, the solutions appeared. All it took was for me to **BE Creative and BE Open to allowing solutions to flow through.** The job was then done with such ease and joy that it made our hearts sing. While building the Institute, we also made an amazing circle of international friends. We shared how to make our favorite dishes and enjoyed reading and sharing our experiences with one another.

Again I learned the power of intention, as well as the value of time. **When an intention becomes your resolve, the results are achieved in no time at all.** I started managing my time in 15-minute chunks, focusing on completing the task every quarter of an hour.

Try out this intention-based way of managing your plans. Use the 15-minute time management approach and you will see for yourself how much you will get done and completed every day. It introduces an even pace to the day and you accomplish what you set out to with ease. Have a go.

African Dictator

Just as the Institute was becoming systemized and routine, I was head-hunted to join the university hospital and take over their computer division. This was when PCs were just emerging, so I had to re-educate myself to understand a very different form of computing. It was great to have had the grounding I'd had, having set up the training programs at the Institute. I applied our training techniques to myself and was able to master ever-newer software systems.

I was in the final phase of rolling out a new medical records system when I received a panicked call from the radiology department, requesting that I check the records of the scans they had taken of a woman who had gone into labor. I rushed over, corrected the glitch and, just as I was leaving, heard the loud groaning of the woman in labor followed by the thump of a fist against the wall and the deep, heavy sigh of a man. I stopped and listened as again and again the same routine repeated. I felt compelled to go towards the labor ward. Just outside the ward there was this big African man, stomping loudly as he was pacing up and down, banging his fist every time the woman in the ward groaned. He would grunt in frustration, letting out a deep guttural sound. His eyes were flaming red, and sweat was pouring down his face. He looked formidable and vulnerable at the same time. His face carried a strange aura of helpless innocence.

I went up to him and offered my hand to him. He grabbed it instantly and held it hard, till it almost hurt. I walked him gently to the waiting room chairs and we sat down. I became ultra-calm, and started breathing deeply and slowly. Soon the African followed my lead and he started to take slow, deep breaths too. The thumping, grunting and sweating subsided as he laid his head on my shoulder. His squeezes of my hand became stronger in response to the rising pace of the labor pains and just when it got to the point where I could have screamed myself, the surgeons and their medical team arrived and I was asked to leave.

I found out later that the man was the Ugandan dictator in exile, Idi Amin, and it was his daughter in labor. She was having a difficult birth. I saw him a few times in the hospital over the next few days; we just exchanged glances and a knowing smile. The experience was an unusual one in a society where men and women are segregated so strictly, so nothing was said publicly about it.

For me it was a major lesson learned. Even a ferocious dictator has feelings. By **BEing Compassion** myself, it made him compassionate, and settled and centered him within his own human beingness. This understanding interrupted my pattern of judging and evaluating people based on my perceptions of their past behaviors.

Is there a time when you did something uncharacteristically compassionate? What did you learn from that experience?

London: *The Hamster on a Hamster Wheel*

We arrived in London at the end of August. I felt like I had come home; everything looked so familiar and so full of life. The natural surroundings, the fun people and their smiles all fueled my spirit of freedom. I loved the independence, the swans, the parks, the Changing of the Guards, the palaces, the castles and the artistry. It captured my heart. Given my experience in advanced IT technologies in Saudi Arabia, I was head-hunted by several recruiting companies and had the pick of jobs to walk into. In the land of the Queen of England, I felt like a queen myself.

We soon bought our first home, with a garden filled with fruit shrubs and roses. Then we bought investment properties. Then we bought even more properties, as well as shares and gold. Life was prosperous, happy, fulfilling and abundant. My optimism was growing at the same pace as my husband's pessimism. I became pregnant and miscarried; we blamed it on my super-demanding job. The frequency of the hitting episodes increased.

The recession arrived, property prices plummeted and my husband was made redundant. I saw it as an opportunity for him to change his career to IT and learn a computer language that was in high demand, since we could not find enough skilled staff. Although he completed the training and got a job even before he finished, exactly as I had predicted, he was becoming more and more depressed. We traveled the world. In China, and behind the Iron Curtain, we traveled the country guided by students, some of whom turned out to be key architects of the revolution that was to follow. In Moscow, we were entertained by the Russian mafia and got to see places where tourists were not allowed to go. Then our son Sai was born.

Just before my maternity leave I undertook an MBA program, intending to stay busy professionally while also being a mother. Of course, everything changed when I became Sai's mom. My baby son became the center of my existence. Still I returned to work and soon after was head-hunted again, this time to head up marketing and IT. That's when I put on the hamster suit.

I was firing on all cylinders. At work, I went from strength to strength. At home I was being a mother to a loving, active, engaging son, while also navigating the extreme Dr. Jekyll and Mr. Hyde episodes with my husband. At times we had a very loving connection, interrupted for no apparent reason by surprisingly hurtful physical assaults, which were then followed by another set of romantic gestures. I understood that my husband was projecting his frustration and anger, aggression followed by remorse, and that I was the object of that expression.

Meanwhile, I was spinning away on the hamster wheel, juggling all of these highly demanding responsibilities.

The job was OK, not fulfilling. I decided to enter the dragons' den with a pitch to create a new organization, one that bridged the gap between IT and the Board, so business strategy could leverage the developments in technology. The project was sanctioned by the Board and the business was created with more than £500,000 in revenues even before it was launched.

The media went crazy over it and I became the voice for the "Bridge between IT and the Board," an unlikely yet real achievement that I had not envisioned. It became a strong foundation for what was to happen next.

Miracles in Divorce

My career was developing well and my role as a mother was now more stabilized and gave me a lot of joy. My role as a wife was disappointing and my dream of a loving marriage until death us do part was crumbling rapidly. The hitting incidents became frequent and continued for the 10 years that we were married. They became more intense during the last four years of our lives together, reaching a peak during my pregnancy.

On the one hand he was the most loving, caring and accommodating husband, and on the other, his frustration and pessimism were so difficult to snap out of, that his anger became uncontrollable. He expressed himself through passive aggression as well as through physical violence. I still felt deep love and care for him and decided to stand by him, no matter what.

I did not share my situation with anyone, though my friends and the people at work did notice my enhanced use of make-up and the big bouquets of red roses that arrived at work after each eruption of violence at home.

After every incident he would become the most loving, caring husband and ask me why I had made him do this to me. I genuinely started to believe that there was something wrong with me. (Later, when I was going through the divorce, I found out that this is a standard expression of most wife-beaters. The perpetrator makes the victim an accomplice.)

I had a child and standing in the corporate world. So the situation at home made me **BE a powerful leader** at work, an amazing problem-solver who thought out of the box. The entrepreneur was born. I reconnected with my earlier choices to **BE Strong, BE Independent and BE Knowing that I am safe and taken care of.** The experience of surviving and thriving in my workplace despite what was going on at home made it possible for me to enter a flourishing life, once I finally chose to step away from the marriage.

In retrospect, this period of being married to and receiving the violent behavior of my childhood sweetheart provided many gifts. They have made my life enchanting ever since. My experience leaving the marriage and what happened afterwards reinforced my belief that miracles are indeed possible and can become the norm. The choice is mine to make. **BE Choice** in the matter, I decided.

I also see that in holding it all in, not sharing what I was going through and BEing Strong physically, I was in fact becoming a victim and crushing my own self-worth at a cellular level. As I became a reliable supporter for others in fulfilling their desires and dreams, I became more and more disconnected from what it was that I wanted for myself.

There were many gifts from this episode in my life and I would not change a single thing about it. I became an entrepreneur, I learned to live and thrive in a different culture and I became resourceful, grateful and experienced luxurious living that I had not seen before. I developed skills, talents and experiences that enabled me to work and live in any part of the world. I learned that I always have a choice in the matter and I am always choosing, even if I choose to make no choice.

Many miracles emerged from this experience. I remain eternally grateful for the birth of my son Sai and for his role in protecting, inspiring and lifting me to step into my unique magnificence and walk my path. It was Sai who first taught me to meditate, under a tree in Regent's Park. In sharing his insights (I called them "Saiisms"), he finally got me to listen to my inner guidance.

When he was just two and half years old, it was Sai who came to my rescue. While playing in the courtyard with his cousin one day, he remarked to my father, "I don't like my dad any more... he hits my mom all the time." (Although there had never been any hitting incidents in front of our son, I realized then that children *know*. They feel the energy.) Sai's revelation came at a time when I had escaped to be with my family, right after a particularly violent incident at home in London. My parents were shocked and asked me to tell it all. It was then that I decided to get the divorce.

The other amazing miracle for which I remain deeply grateful came in the form of my temp PA (personal assistant), Audrey. She was a trained barrister and had been temping as a PA due to a deep recession in the U.K. at the time, when law firms were not hiring interns. I now believe she was planted there by my spirit guides.

Every time I received the large bouquet of red roses after a violent episode at home, Audrey would say, "Let me know if I can help in any way. What you are going through often happens in my community." I would reply, embarrassed, "Thanks, but I don't know what you are referring to." In my heart, though, I felt comforted that someone understood.

So finally, when I told her what had happened and that I was going to ask for a divorce, she explained the whole legal procedure that would enable us to have police protection, as well as get the divorce within three weeks. She arranged for the best lawyers and barristers and also secured legal aid for the entire process to be subsidized. She orchestrated everything I needed to be able to achieve the divorce within the three weeks, with police protection. The only catch was that during that time I could not have any contact with people we knew together as a couple and absolutely *no* contact with my husband. So my son and I stayed at a YMCA and I managed my team of over 50 people from the corporate HQ of one of my Board directors. All worked out perfectly. I got divorced and had police protection for over two years. I took all the financial responsibility for everything, so we could rebuild our lives **BEing Optimistic**, positive and exercising our freedom of choice.

I also learned that the opposite of love is not hate, it is indifference. At no point during this whole phase did I experience hate. I shifted from a state of victimhood because I felt called to **BEing Free and to making an empowered choice.**

I went through a wide range of emotions as I settled into my new life as a single parent while also being the thriving owner of a rapidly-expanding business. By **choosing to BE** I realized that what could have become a burdensome and traumatic situation became instead a task to be managed and handled with efficiency. Hence the job was done and life flourished far beyond what I could ever have predicted or planned.

Is there an area in your life where you can now shift away from DO and choose to just BE? Apply some of my lessons here and notice the difference that they make. BEing is believing in your own innate strength. When you do this that strength is activated and energized, ready for directed action. Try it out, you will be pleasantly surprised.

Hamster on Three Hamster Wheels

In my new life as a working single parent, I spent every spare moment I had with my son. I remained very actively engaged in his schoolwork and extracurricular activities, from horse riding, rowing and violin to piano, sport and drama. In parallel, my business was growing and becoming very visible and profiled in the media. It was backed and actively supported by 90 of the top 100 companies in the UK. It received large sums in grants from the EU, too, to create the innovative business and learning environments of the 21st century.

Life was hectic and getting busier, as I went from one surprising success to another. I had an adoring lover in Peter who enjoyed being a father to Sai. He would often say, "One day, you will understand how much I love you and will feel trusting enough to share what you want with me." I knew he loved me for who I was and I was learning to trust him as a dad for Sai. We supported each other in business and were jointly recognized as leading innovators in the information and communication technology space in Europe. Our projects won several international awards and accolades.

I was called to speak alongside major pioneers in technology and advocates of the "Information Superhighway," including US Vice President Al Gore, Marc Andreessen the founder of Netscape, Peter Drucker, Arthur C. Clarke, Guy Kawasaki, Tim Berners-Lee the founder of the world wide web, and many Silicon Valley inventors, captains of industry and political personalities. Suddenly, I had to stop myself in my tracks.

Was I truly achieving what I had set out to achieve? No. It was time for me to move on to the next challenge: the gap in the market and, in British industry, the gap in inspired leadership. I sold the business I had founded. Then the hamster stepped into the cage and onto the hamster wheel.

I formed the Inspired Leaders Network and started spinning the wheel again, gaining momentum. I attracted the top, the biggest, the most innovative, the very best in inspired leadership; they were game changers from around the world. Our Network became a standard-setter and was commissioned by the UK government to create the Inspired Leaders Index. Almost all of the London Times' top 100 organizations became clients. Peter left his organization and joined me as an equal partner in making our mark, transforming leadership in British industry. While still on the rise with Inspired Leaders, I was drawn into the glitzy world of movies. I became a film producer as well, producing Bollywood, Tamil and English movies in factory style: one in development, one in pre-production, one on the floor and one in post-production.

Now the hamster was on two wheels, spinning at the speed of light (at least it felt that way). I often said to myself, "So here we go again; where is *this* going to lead?" This crazy cycle was finally interrupted by some catastrophic news via a call I received when I was in India for the release of our mega-star cast Bollywood movie. The call was from my son and I rushed back to be by the side of my partner Peter. He had suffered a major stroke and was in the acute brain injury unit.

Everything stopped. The Inspired Leaders Network was sold to one of our founding members. The movie production business was closed, just as soon as our set of 15 movies was completed. Just before the global financial markets meltdown, I did manage to get into high-prestige real estate development, which turned out to be a case of rather bad timing.

It was a perfect storm: my hamster-on-a-wheel pattern was interrupted, and I had a brief moment of reflection as I readjusted to the reality of the situation and its effect on our lives.

Peter, who had been a powerful corporate CEO and top-level advisor to the UK and EU governments, would never work again. His life and his personality had changed forever. In many ways it was for the best, though it certainly took its toll on me and introduced me to a new career of being a full-time caregiver and bread-earner for the family. I was on three hamster wheels now: in my relationship at home, with Peter and as a family; attempting to minimize the impact of the global financial market crash on our affairs; and keeping up with a superfast growth spike in my business. I could not just stop what I was doing; I had to step into lateral entrepreneurial thinking mode again, and create the next phase of my life.

Rising From the Ashes Over the Rainbow

It was Christmas of 2007 when Sai decided to take a gap year in India, to become a dating coach and stock trader. Peter and I went to our usual place, on the north shore of Oahu in Hawaii. This time, we decided to travel there with a stop through California, where we took the picturesque Highway 1 drive to our favorite hotel in Big Sur, The Post Ranch Inn. When we arrived, we chose the perfect tree house suite, hanging over the cliffs above the ocean. Peter decided to go for a massage and I chose a different treatment from the menu: something called "Destiny Retrieval" with a "shamanic high priest." I was determined to use this time to find a way forward that served us and was sustainable.

I arrived at the yoga yurt for the treatment and found that I was there by myself. I waited, half expecting to see a Peruvian priest show up in full regalia. Then in walked Jon, in a T-shirt and shorts. I felt dejected and wanted to leave, until he spoke softly but firmly to me, explaining what I was to experience in the two hours I was to spend with him. He changed into his priestly attire, and asked me to choose from his divine bag of natural treasures. He then created a circular mandala and invited me to lie down while he performed a ritual, invoking various spirits of nature.

I must have gone into a trance, because the next thing I remember experiencing were his words declaring my destiny. He said I was among the two percent of people in the world whose job it is to dream new worlds into being. He told me that my dreaming was necessary, and that the Earth was preparing for its next incarnation. He also shared that my ancestors were with me, blessing and protecting me and sometimes getting impatient with me. So far I had been unable to complete the dreaming that the Divine had planned for me to bring about.

All this language seemed very strange to me, though I felt very calm and powerful in a gentle yet certain way. Jon guided me to create an altar for my ancestors and to get on with dreaming the new world. He also gave me the experience of working with spirits of nature by going for walks and collecting objects that called out to me and creating a mandala, working with each object one at a time to understand what it wanted to show me or communicate to me. It seemed like a weird thing to do, but hey, I was going to be in Hawaii, on the ocean for three weeks, so I could easily do this. He said it would de-clutter my field and minimize any confusion that I may have had about the way forward. And once I received the communication from the object, I was to release it into the ocean.

We arrived in Hawaii and felt like we had come home. After my Bikram yoga I would go out for a walk and collect the objects; I had created a big mandala on our deck on the beach. I was following guidance as suggested by Jon and released a lot of baggage from unsaid communications from various relationships including my ex-husband, my family members, my co-directors and some difficult members of my team. I was just starting to see the benefit of doing this kind of work — a ray of light was indeed visible at the end of this tunnel of dark shadow stuff that I was walking through — when the unpredictable happened.

We had our own masseuse, Katie, who would come over and work with us when we arrived in Oahu. She was massaging me one day, when she suddenly stopped and said, "I would never do this normally, but you have to see this, this is a sign." I came off the massage table and there it was: a full rainbow. Above the rainbow was a cloud formation and in the middle of that cloud was another cloud, rising from it, shaped like a phoenix. I called out to Peter, my head started spinning and I felt dizzy. I thought I might be blacking out with excitement. Peter brought his digital camera and took a photo. We all saw the photo — which included the tree from our front yard in it. The portion of the tree that was photographed had two breast-like knots jutting out from its trunk; they were very majestic, proud and perfectly formed. Katie saw the photo and went pale.

She held our hands and said, "Thank you for all you have been for me, I am sorry to say that this is the last time I will see you two together."

"Why are you saying this, Katie?" I asked.

She replied, "Look at the photo, Mynoo. It's a premonition of what's to come. You are emerging as a goddess, rising like a phoenix from the ashes, riding over the rainbow. There is no Peter here, this is a blessing from the Universe of the beauty you are to experience. Do not reject it, receive it, allow it to flow and accept the divine gifts that come with this experience."

I was confused. Peter and I looked at each other, and my heart felt at the same time a hollowness and a knowing that there was something to take note of in what she was saying. I became restless and I realized this was a part of the destiny retrieval process that Jon had initiated at The Post Ranch Inn.

We returned to London. I felt that I had carried a constant undertone of restlessness from that ride over the rainbow in Hawaii. The destiny retrieval with Jon, which had connected me to the light, kept being interrupted by this ongoing feeling of restlessness.

I chose to **BE Present** as that was the only way to overcome that feeling and create an opening, so I could also **BE Certain** that all would turn out perfectly at the right time and in the right order. This choice paved the way for me to finally step off the hamster wheels.

Have you had nature show you signs that
you wish you had taken on board?

CHAPTER 5:

BE CONNECTED

The Berlin Wall Moment

On my return to London I realized that the hamster suit was still on; even though I was off the wheel, I remained in the cage. I formed a new business: a niche, high-performance consultancy for enterprises with an iconic brand potential. I invited my mentor and my coach to join me as partners in the venture and off we went. Within months, the businesses we were working with started doubling and even tripling their turnover.

It was exciting to see what was possible and as this success grew I began going deeper and deeper into the dark night of my soul. I knew I had stepped back onto the hamster wheel again and this time, I had had enough. I did not know where was next for me. I did not know who I was or what I even wanted — I just knew that it was not more of the same. Something dramatic had to shift, and I had no idea how to do it.

I knew then that I was at a pivotal point in my life, all the aspects of my life felt stressed and stretched to the max. I had to make a choice. On one side of the pivot, the choice would be coming from fear; on the other side, the choice would be coming from love. I was facing a moment of two different world-realities.

"It's my own Berlin Wall moment," I thought, as I posted on my first-ever blog, asking this question: The world changed forever when the Berlin Wall came down; before that moment the Cold War was a reality, and after it, there was no Cold War anymore. The world had been polarized, pro-Cold War or not, and after the wall came down, every country had to readjust. Do we have our own Berlin Wall moments, when our world changes forever and every aspect of our life has to readjust? With this question I ended my post on 29th December 2009.

Can you recall a moment in your life that was like a Berlin Wall moment for you, when the reality of the world as you had known it changed forever? How did you respond?

Alternative New Year

A few days later I called my friend Ellen, an intuitive who lived on the east coast of the US and had the gift of tuning into spirit guides. Each year I would consult her about the year ahead. That year I asked her what my guides had to say to me about the following year. Much to my surprise, Ellen went ballistic. It was as if she could not stop talking. She asserted that my guides wanted to communicate with me and that my head was too full. I had to stop everything I was doing and go away; to go away without Peter or Sai for at least three weeks, to somewhere near the ocean but not next to it, somewhere with lots of trees. She repeated herself several times, each time asking whether I had heard exactly what had been said. It was important and urgent. I should not ignore this. I felt so overwhelmed that I disconnected the call.

At that point I had consulted with Ellen for over seven years and had never met her. I felt that she did not understand my life and the pressures I felt I was under. We had a very large mortgage. Peter's health condition was challenging and his level of dependency was growing. I was under tremendous pressure to maintain the performance of my clients' businesses, which were going from success to success. I simply did not believe I could just go away for three weeks.

What I did decide to do was to have a different type of New Year's Eve. I invited my online network of friends to join me in my home for an alternative New Year, bringing it in with a chant of *"Om Namah Shivaya"*. I asked Peter and Sai to go by themselves to visit the friends with whom we usually celebrated New Year's Eve.

That evening, 32 people showed up with food, champagne and yummy non-alcoholic drinks. I knew only five of them. One of the women who came was a jazz singer turned voice healer. She had lived in the ashram in India with Guru Maya for over three years. She arrived with her harmonium and drums and led the *"Om Namah Shivaya"* chant at midnight. We all chose our special message for the New Year from the deck of goddess cards, which had been one of my Christmas gifts that year. No champagne was opened. We were all ecstatically high on the energy of the experience itself, without alcohol.

We created our intentions for the year ahead and then, as a group, we went on a rampage of appreciation. It just went on and on, and as it did, we became more and more intrigued by what the next year had in store for each one of us. At 3:00 am Peter and Sai arrived home. They felt that they must have missed out on a great party as we were all still there, drinking in the sweet elixir of appreciating and feeling appreciated, acknowledged and supremely grateful.

That New Year's Eve celebration was my way of making a choice coming from love. I had moved, pivoting from fear to love. I felt great in my heart. It began to snow as the sun rose and we all went to bed.

Put the Right Foot Forward

On the 3rd of January I woke up with my right ankle swollen like an elephant's foot and on fire, pulsating and burning hot. We called an ambulance; I was rushed into the hospital, taken in to emergency care and seen by the doctor straight away. My feet were put on a sling in the air and I had two strong intravenous antibiotic drips. The consultant arrived several hours later and explained that what I had was a small infection called cellulitis, where a particular bacteria attaches under the top layer of the skin. In this region, the capillaries are too fine to provide sufficient blood supply and the infection aggravates quickly.

In my case, it was an extreme situation. I had to be prepared to be on this treatment for three to six months. "What...?" I simply could not believe what I had heard. I called my American intuitive; it was too much of a coincidence for this to have happened so soon after our conversation.

When Ellen heard what had taken place, she was unfazed. She said, "Well... right ankle, that's you knowing that you have to move forward and you're just not doing it. Stop with the stubbornness. Make the choice to go away for three weeks, and the infection will subside."

I put the phone down, thinking, "OK, whatever." My veins were already starting to close up and the doctors had to look for fresh veins in painful and unusual places (on my feet, for instance).

I shared the gist of my conversation with Peter and Sai and they both agreed with Ellen that I should go away. Finally, three days later, I made the choice. I would go to Bali and stay in a resort that my best friend from London and another friend from the US had recommended. They had each stayed there by themselves. Within a few hours of having made the choice and ordering my flight tickets, the infection began to subside. Within a few days I was discharged from the hospital, with a supply of oral antibiotics for a month.

I chose to put my right foot forward, choosing to walk my path coming from a space of love. **I had broken the cycle of fear that had made me a hamster on a wheel. This cycle was now severed forever; the hamster suit was off. I stepped out of the cage free and ready to start over,** feeling vulnerable and excited about what was to come.

So...

BE Learning and BE Knowing

Just like me, you have had your own experiences growing up. I did not realize how formative they had been in shaping and providing direction to my life. Episodes that I thought were negative are actually rich in their own gifts, providing a strong foundation for where I am headed now.

> *Consider your own journey and look for the gifts, learnings and blessings that have emerged from it. Consider all manner of experiences and incidents. Now it's time to digest them.*

> *Digestion is a three-part process: ingestion, absorption and excretion. You have already ingested your life experience, now it's time to absorb the nutrients (i.e. learnings) and release the rest. I invite you to take your time as you look at the good, the bad, and the ugly; you will find the beautiful.*

PART TWO:

GLOWING UP

In this part you join me in the journey of going within myself, where I got to know WHO I AM and WHAT I AM TO DO NEXT. This was the biggest rollercoaster ride of my life; it was completely unpredictable and full of surprises, like the cave of wonders from *Aladdin*. I discovered treasures of all different kinds. I started writing and became a prolific vessel for the cosmic wisdom that started flowing through me.

If you are like I was in the material "real world," then you may become confused or may not understand as you follow me through what happened there. I was in exactly the same place. I too tried hard to comprehend it, and to figure out what was taking place. My logical mind did not have a way to explain it, as it was not something I knew about or understood. Now that it was happening to me, I could not deny its existence. I finally decided to let go of trying to understand what was going on. I chose to BE Receiving and learning from the wisdom that was being gifted to me and through me for the world. I chose to BE Present to enjoy the moments, and to experience all that was occurring.

CHAPTER 6:

BE EXTRAORDINARY

Bali Happened to Me

I had agreed to go to Bali for three weeks, by myself. It felt strange, and I was anxious. I checked in with Ellen, my American intuitive friend, as this was such an unusual occurrence in my life; I felt I needed guidance of a different kind. My spirit guides, communicating through her, guided me to focus on only two questions during my time in Bali and they were: "Who am I?" and "What I am to do next?"

"Who am I?" I did not understand what that was about at all. I was certain I already knew who I was, so I dismissed it. What I wanted to do next, however, sounded like a fun brainstorming to do on my vacation.

I had to find a way to fill my days, three weeks felt like a very long time to focus on these two questions. At my mother's suggestion, I decided to do a yoga camp with Baba Ramdev from India. It happened to be available in London, on the weekend just before I was due to depart for Bali. I learned yoga, pranayama, chanting and meditation.

After a 21-hour journey, I arrived in Bali. I got to my room and slept for a day and a half. The resort was beautiful, filled with coconut palms and overlooking the rice fields. My bedroom was in the middle of the fields and from the bed I had an amazing view of treetops, spectacular cloud formations and breathtaking sunsets.

When I emerged from my deep rest, I found out that for two out of the three weeks I was to be the only guest in the resort. My first reaction was that I had to move to another hotel. Then I decided to stay put and created a daily routine of long stretches of yoga, pranayama, chanting, goddess card guidance and journaling, followed by brainstorming what I wanted to do next. I decided that I would read my brainstorm lists after seven days, so that I would have something to look forward to.

Day 7 arrived, and I was excited. After breakfast it was time to look at the lists I had created. There were 23 pages of them, so lots to reflect and choose from. I was thrilled. When the time arrived and I started reading the lists, turning page after page, my heart started to sink. At one point I felt like someone had hit me, hard, with a sledgehammer. A dam burst open and tears started rolling down my cheeks. I was not consciously crying, but I could not control the tears gushing from my eyes. My vision became blurry, and as I fought to see through the teary eyes, a sense of desperation set in. I could not find a single thing I had written that I wanted to do for *myself*. The list was all about me and Peter, me and Sai, us as a family, Mom, Dad, my sisters.

I stopped turning the pages, wiped my tears away and looked up at the sky, as if asking for some divine help. "What do *I* want to do next?" I asked myself. "What color do I want to see, what music do I want to hear? Do I want to dance or sing or jump? What, what, *what*?" I was desperately seeking and searching for something inside. My mind just remained blank. Nothing, just nothing came up. I felt like my heart was gripped by hopelessness, and a sense of fear took hold. I could feel the resonance of the urgency that was present in Ellen's voice when she had said to me, "Go away *NOW* for three weeks."

"What happened?" I asked myself. "WHO AM I?" At some point in the last 49 years I had just lost that connection to me, and my life had become about supporting everyone else on *their* paths.

I decided right then that it was time for me to connect to me. However, I still did not know what to do with "WHO AM I?" or even where to start with that question. So I decided to focus the next day on choosing what I was to do next. The heaviness in my heart eased somewhat.

The resort had a business library, and the next day I decided to take over that library; I was, after all, the only guest there. I chose to do all my morning routines and rituals in the library and on the terrace outside of it. I committed to myself that I was not going to leave there until I had made my choice. As I did my morning practices and entered the block of time that I was to meditate, I saw clearly what I wanted to do next.

I saw that throughout my life I had made choices, created boundaries and prioritized different aspects of my life from a place of trying to manage expectations, and I had compromised my own needs in the process.

In an effort to keep peace and try to please everyone, I had often become overwhelmed. I continued to appear strong on the surface while, unbeknownst to me, I had weakened on the inside and then allowed myself to disconnect from within. I realized that I HAD MADE THESE CHOICES and that I had led a life of stress, anxiety and disconnectedness.

So NOW I would make a different choice: I chose to live an EXTRAORDINARY LIFE, where all aspects of my life can and do coexist with ease, grace and joy. This was the next phase of my life. And so it is. I felt it, and wrote it down. Then I experienced this absolutely beautiful sensation of every cell in my being coming alive.

The cloud was lifted, darkness left behind and I emerged from the library, BEing Clear, Certain, Gracious and in Joy. Beaming from ear to ear, with a flutter in my heart and a spring in my step. I was so pleased. I felt plugged in, I was into me and it was only a matter of time before I would uncover WHO I AM. Now I was certain of that.

Living the Extraordinary Life

I was blissed out, chilled out and ecstatically excited all at once; it felt like I had finally cracked the BEing Me code. A tremendous sense of accomplishment came over me. I ordered the papaya with lime and sat under the bale (an Indonesian pagoda) that had been infused through Feng Shui with the energy of wood, and the question of WHAT. I heaved a big, deep sigh, looked up at the sky and suddenly felt that I had been brought straight back down to earth. A frown formed on my forehead and my smile changed to a contemplative, somber expression.

"Hmmm, so what does it mean, practically, living this extraordinary life? How do I do this? How will I know that I am on track?" All the typical left-brain questions came flooding in. In the last seven days I had spent in Bali, I had experienced a glimmer of living this way. This is what I wanted and I was going to have it. I resorted to my old companion, BE Certain, to come from intention. *"Do what keeps you in flow and you got it,"* was the intuitive answer I received. This was all well and good, but I required something specific and practical that I could put into practice every day.

I could not think of anyone who lived in this way who could serve as a role model for me. It occurred to me that I was good, in fact among the best in the field, at converting ideas into businesses. This was an idea that I wanted to make real so I chose, in that moment, to become a consultant to me: Project Extraordinary Life. And by the next day I was going to have a plan of action to make this real. *That's done.* I felt the resolve energy and enjoyed experiencing the shift in my cellular chemistry as I emerged from being committed to living an extraordinary life to becoming resolved that this is so. *Done.*

I woke up early, completed my morning practices, collected lots of blank sheets of paper and tore them up into little square pieces to be used as a replacement for Post-It notes. I entered the library, excited and anticipating a perfect outcome. I decided to jot down on each little square one thing that I had done at some point in my life that had made my life great. I was on a roll and wrote down 49 such things. OK, so that was a large number of items to choose from! So I decided to combine the selection process with meditation, in order to distill the perfect ones for this next phase of my life.

As luck would have it, I found a small blob of Blu-Tack on one of the shelves in the library. (I have never found this in Bali, so I like to believe it was brought there just for me to do this work.) I now had 49 little squares, stuck on books and shelves all around me. I sat in the middle of them, put on my stopwatch and started meditating. This was the first time in my life I was meditating without a timer alarm, just a stopwatch. I was still curious to know how long it took for me to be able to arrive at the action choices. I meditated for one hour and twenty-three minutes and opened my eyes. I knew I had gone somewhere very deep, connecting to the essence of my soul.

I began to stare at each little note that I had written. I was looking for which of these actions had made the difference between my life being great or my life being extraordinary, where more than one aspect of my life had coexisted harmoniously. And there it was, as if by magic: I had a strange experience when six little squares with my writings on them just popped out, like a hologram. I went to each of them, one by one, and pulled them off the wall.

Now I had my plan of action, my six pillars to living an extraordinary life with ease, grace and joy. I knew what each of these actions entailed; I had done them before and had forgotten about the power they held. This time, I was going to do these six actions every single day for the next 12 months. Something big was bound to shift and, in the process of being on this practically-directed journey, I would find the answer to WHO AM I? I felt certain, active and resolved.

I also knew the secret **that I was going to BE Extraordinary living my life, to BE Ease, BE Joy and BE Grace.** I now had a practical set of actions to support me in getting there, every day. I put on my dancing shoes and stepped on to my path. It was now illuminated and I knew how to navigate myself to get there. I felt whole and complete.

True Romance

I came out of the library, sipping on a fresh young coconut from the tree, feeling pleased at what I had accomplished, ready and raring to go with my action plan. This time **I was going to BE the six pillars, not DO them,** as I would have done in the past. I was curious to see the effects. I still had just over a week in Bali to put this into practice. I felt serene, in joy and at peace.

That's when I noticed that something had changed. The resort felt chaotic; suddenly there was a lot of activity and stressed-out Balinese servers rushing around. I asked what was going on and they said that there was a whole group coming into the resort the next day, for a week-long entrepreneurs' business mastery program.

What?! Just when I had my solution, I would be seduced into distractions. I was being presented with what I loved most – business and entrepreneurs – to hang out with. I had been deprived of this for over two weeks now. It was a dilemma; I felt conflicted and confused.

I called Ellen, who by this point had become my lifeline. "Should I move to another resort?" I asked her. My guides said, *"No, stay put. Don't share about your business background, talk about what you are here for and receive the blessings."* I was told that there were people coming there bearing gifts for me, and that if I was in the right tuning with nature, the Universe had a surprise that it had been waiting for me to be ready to receive. These gifts and the surprise were an important component of the next phase of my journey. I like surprises, so I stayed put.

By the first night the resort was full. I was asked by the hotel staff if I would like to join the group for dinner and I did. I sat next to a beautiful lady from Perth, Australia. She asked me who I was, and what I was doing there. I shared that I was finding myself, searching for who I am and what I am to do next. She in turn shared that she had a healing and spiritual practice in Perth, and that she would like to gift me a process that she used to help people find and walk their path. "Aha, my first gift! I am liking this," I thought. I thanked her and we all dispersed into our rooms.

Dolphin Avatar

The next day, after my morning practice, I came down for breakfast. The entrepreneurs' class was on; the conference room was heaving with action and knowledge. I just quietly walked past it and felt like something or someone had darted out of the conference room and was following me. I turned around to look, and an elegant lady was beaming at me, waving and gesturing for me to stop. I did. She came up to me and held the wrist of my right hand and asked me to follow her. In a strange tone of voice she urged me to abide and I did. It felt surreal and I felt somehow safe. I could not logically explain the desire in me to follow instructions from a stranger I had just briefly seen.

We went to another bale on the grounds of the resort. She sat me down and said that she had been guided to work with me and help me find my ocean avatars; I needed to connect with their gifts for the next stage I was being prepared for. WOW! Another gift! I was happy, and I allowed her to guide me into a deep sea meditation. She took me into a trance and we stepped into the energy of the ocean. She took me deep, deep, deep into the depths of this dark sea where I saw the dolphins, reaching out and beckoning me to join in their play. I felt that they *were* me and I connected instantly to the essence of these dolphins.

I saw a pure white light beaming from the dolphins into me, making us one. She gently brought me out of this amazing experience and said that I now had the dolphins as my guides; so if I am stuck, or have unanswered questions, I can tune into the energy of the dolphins and they will have the perfect response to support my every need. It felt good (though my left-brain logic was perplexed). I decided to go with the flow and gratefully receive the gift with which I had just been blessed.

I felt like I had done a deep, hard workout. I guessed that in the realm of spirit, I had hacked through, cut open and released a lot of toxicity that no longer served me. Though my physical body felt a bit strained, my heart was open and my mind was calm, knowing that all was well. I realized that I was to just BE Well, accepting the flow that was to unlock after this experience. I felt such a profound shift that I spent the rest of the day just being with myself. I ordered room service and had an early night.

I woke up early the next day feeling vibrant and raring to go. The beaming lady had connected me to the dolphins. I knew immediately that they were there to support me. It felt very "woo woo" and also quite real as an experience to go through. Again I found myself blissed out, chilled out and ecstatically excited all at once. I felt like I had cracked open a shield, that under the guise of "protection" had previously shut out these wondrous revelations.

I completed my yoga and exercises and with a large glass of water I sat down to pick the goddess card for the day. The card that I pulled out was Goddess Guinevere: *True Romance.* "The universe has heard the stirrings of your heart and is delivering your true love to you..." it said.

"I am already with my soulmate Peter," I thought to myself. "I think this is a mistake." I tried again and the card I pulled out this time was Goddess Guinevere. "Hmmm, this can't be right, let's have another go," I thought, and again the card I pulled out, for the third time, was Goddess Guinevere. "There must be some mistake here." I put the Guinevere card away, out of the deck, and tried a fourth time. This time, the card I pulled was Goddess Green Tara: *Purify. Stay away from toxic relationships and toxic environments. You are more sensitive than usual at the moment so purify...* "Ah, well, let's get on with the day," I told myself, as one of the most surprising days of my life began to unfold.

By this point in the day I was ravenously hungry and went up to the cafe. The beaming elegant lady was at the bar. "I am waiting for you," she said.

I did not feel like I wanted to speak with anyone. Something strange was unfolding within me that I could not put into words.

She came closer to me and said, "You are not doing it, are you?"

"What am I not doing?" I asked.

She said, "You are not asking the dolphins for help with your problem."

"Which problem? I don't understand."

She said, "OK, then let's go down into the ocean again and let them show it to you."

I felt weak, but allowed her to take me through the trance routine again. This time the ocean was still and very dark for a while; then I saw an image. I moved closer to see what I was being shown: I saw two dolphins, a big one and a smaller one right next to it. They were just still and sad, not moving; I sensed that they were just there, figuring something out. Then suddenly the smaller dolphin moved away and rolled in the water, blowing bubbles, and swam away from the big one. As if by magic, the big one became frisky too and started swimming out into the ocean. I followed it and saw it feeling happy, meeting new friends. The smaller one reappeared looking happy and playful too, and it swam away in another direction, doing its own thing. I was ready to rise up from the ocean now. The message communicated to me by these creatures, though surprising, was loud and clear: It was time for me to return, to complete my relationship with Peter.

We were both ready to embark on the next phase of our lives. For that we would have to step away from each other, allowing ourselves to express who we are to the world, fully, with complete freedom and joy. There was nothing wrong with our relationship; it was just complete, and time to move on to what was next in store for each of us. If we ignored this message, then we would wind up feeling stuck, depleted of life force and sinking down like a heavy lead stone, until we would prematurely depart from the planet.

Stuck, lifeless and depleted, or vibrant, vital and free? The choice was simple and the dolphins had given me the gift of making that choice. The lady brought me out of the meditation and I found that I was at peace, in complete harmony with my soul. I told her that what I had been shown and told by the dolphins came as a bit of a shock, but was a revelation of something that should have been obvious. I had seen what I needed to and now I had to get into action about it. I expressed my gratitude to her, returned to my room and went to bed. After a long time I slept soundly, with no dreams at all, at a different level of depth. When I woke up it was as if I were 10 years younger, filled with energy and vibrant vitality like never before. Wow... where did all this energy come from? I just welcomed it, and dressed up for dinner that night.

So...

BE Extraordinary

*What can you choose today that will support you to
BE Extraordinary and to live your life with ease, grace and joy?*

*What can you stop tolerating today that
gets in the way of you coming alive?*

*What can you be eternally grateful for? What can generate
feelings of appreciation within you every day?*

*What one word that diminishes your power
will you stop using, starting today?*

CHAPTER 7:

BE JOY

Aha! The Suprise has Arrived...

I was early for dinner, so I found a quiet enclave surrounded by coconut palms and sat in the middle of it to meditate. I went straight into the zone, feeling a deep connection to the trees. I realized that trees are OK no matter what; even if they are chopped down, they just allow it to be. They have an inner knowing that their true nature is in service to Mother Earth and to humanity and all living things at large. I asked the trees to envelop me in their OK-ness. I came out of this meditation with a strange flutter of excitement in my heart, as if there was something special waiting for me that night.

We were all seated around this magnificent table setting, under the moonlit, star-filled night sky of Bali. I was sitting next to a Japanese hairdresser. Our conversation kept being interrupted by an obnoxious, self-obsessed Scandinavian hippie, who was sitting across the table from us and constantly asking the Japanese hairdresser to fix a time to cut his pony tail off. She kept avoiding him and after a few minutes he would shout out her name and ask again. He was extremely annoying. We finally decided to ignore him and shut him out of our vision, and be just as rude. I don't recall how it happened, but I must have gone into a reverie and when I returned, I found that he and I were the only people left at the table.

I picked up my stuff and started walking away, fast, to get to my room. This guy ran ahead of me and came and stood right in front of me, with his face uncomfortably close to mine. He asked in a loud alpha male voice, "Who ARE you?" I decided to go professional and gave him my impressive business and movie profile. I rattled it off with aggressive assertion. There was silence and he remained still, engaged, looking piercingly into my eyes and said, "That is all fine, but WHO ARE YOU?"

Hmmmmm. I came back to my senses. I chose to BE Certain and in flow again and I told him what I should have shared in the first place: "I am here to find myself and what I am to do next."

He brightened up and said, with childlike excitement, "You must follow me to my bedroom."

"Why?" I asked.

"I want to give you something," he said.

"What?" I reacted.

"A bed of nails," he said.

"A bed of nails, like the fakirs use in India?" I clarified.

"Yes, based on the same philosophy, you sleep on this and after the first 10 minutes you cross the pain threshold and go into a deep healing. I think this will help you in your quest."

Made sense: guess he wasn't so obnoxious after all. We stopped by his bedroom and he gave me a Shakti mat, a yoga mat of sorts with 325 little plastic nails on it. "Try it. Here is the booklet, and if it's too painful, return it to me, no offense taken." I thanked him and went to my room.

After a hot bath and my night chanting meditation, I lay on the mat. It was painful! I put it away, wondering what I had been thinking. I went back to bed. At 4:00 am I was woken up, as if something was in the room. I sat up and my inner guidance asked me to use the mat

(I had begun following my inner guidance at this point). This time, I followed the 90-minute routine described in the booklet. After I finished it all, I decided to rest for a few minutes on my comfy bed before waking up to do my morning practices. Then something I had not envisaged happened.

I dove into a deep, deep sleep for over five hours. In that time I had three vivid dreams. In each one I experienced a distinct emotion that built up and built up to get to an intense crescendo and just then the dream changed, like a scene from a movie, and the new emotion stepped in.

The first of the emotions I dealt with was fear; in my dream I had caught a murderer red-handed and he and his cronies were climbing up the fire escape to kill me. Just when they got to the door and banged it open, the dream changed. The next emotion was an intense sensual experience with a divine soul and this too built up to a peak when the dream changed. The last emotion to set in was intense frustration, about something I wanted to say, and it kept coming up to my throat and I was unable to voice it. This dream had Peter in it and my head was bursting at what I wanted to say to him and I just could not get it out of my mouth. Right when I got to the point in my dream where I mustered up all the courage to speak up, I was awake, in shock at what had just occurred. I sat up on the bed, knowing that I had indeed gone through a very deep healing to bring into harmony and balance these three emotions. That mat was mine; I was going to keep it and buy it off the Scandinavian hippie.

That evening we sat next to each other; I agreed that I was going to buy the mat from him. We laughed, shared stories from our lives. Then something weird started to happen. I would speak, giving him an answer to a question he had in his mind and had not voiced; and then he would do the same. We were communicating perfectly, without necessarily saying it all in words. We just knew. On the way back we decided to connect with my son in London; as we sat down to speak with him on Skype, we were both engulfed by waves and waves of hair-raising goosebump moments. My heart was beating fast and I knew this connection was not the usual meeting. There was a fullness to our communication that I had never experienced before. It was like he saw me, got me and understood. We were like old long-lost friends coming together, meeting up and feeling as if nothing had changed. My cells were rejoicing at meeting this old friend. I was happy and feeling good.

I offered to help the group of entrepreneurs with the last part of their business mastery assignment. Afterwards, we came back to the resort, a whole group of us, to celebrate. The Scandinavian hippie, who had by now gotten a haircut, ordered two bottles of Dom Pérignon champagne on the beach. I was not drinking. We were all talking happily when suddenly I tranced out again and when I emerged, what felt like only moments later, I found that there were only the two of us on the beach. Everybody else had gone to bed.

I packed up, ready to go to bed myself, when he said something quite profound. I stopped in my tracks and responded with something equally wise. This deep wisdom exchange continued and I heard myself say a few times, "I can't believe I just said that." We were getting lit up and invigorated by what was coming through us and we kept going until it was sunrise. We were full of energy and beaming with vitality and joy. He returned to fly home to Perth and I went back to my suite with a happy warm feeling in my heart.

I called Ellen that night and asked, "Who is this guy, and what happened last night?" Her first response was, "Aha, the surprise has arrived." My guides went on to explain, *"You are two parts of one soul. You met and recognized each other, and felt complete and energized. You have come together in this lifetime to procreate a template project that is essential for the planet as it emerges into its next era and rebirths itself energetically. Keep your relationship pure and unspoiled. Stay away from physical or sexual activity and allow the magic of your coming together and recognizing each other to unfold. Allow yourself to receive the gifts that are in store for you."* Ellen also asked me to create parameters for our relationship and to share this openly with him, to enable the flow of gifts to begin. I did that and what unfolded took us both by surprise.

Third Eye Opening

As I settled back into the last few days I had left in Bali, I noticed a weird feeling of strong activity in my forehead region. It was as if there were gremlins in there and they were working away, busily cleaning up my forehead, especially the area in between my eyebrows. It felt extremely uneasy and I often sat around holding my forehead in my hands. There was no pain, just this uneasiness.

I called Ellen to ask what was going on. My guides responded through her saying that my third eye was being worked on for a higher purpose. "Third eye, what is that? I'm now going to look as weird as Shiva, the Indian god, with a big open third eye on his forehead," I thought.

So much of what I was experiencing just did not make any sense; I did not understand. I was just starting to allow things to occur and to let go of the desire for it to make logical sense before I took action. I sent an email to my friends asking whether anyone knew what this third eye thing meant. Some of the responses I received I could not comprehend. I still did not know what to do.

One morning just after breakfast, I was sitting there with my forehead in my hands again when the GM of the resort came up to me and asked, "Is your third eye opening?"

"What? Wow, how did you know? Yes I think it is and it's uneasy, what can I do?" I asked.

He said after his duty that day he would take me to his family's spiritual healer, who could do a coconut blessing and that that would help me.

We went to see this Balinese spiritual healer. He was in his home, a very modest place, and he had a sweet, serene presence. I explained in English what was happening and he suggested that I do this yellow coconut blessing for the next three days. He gave the ingredients to the GM, who was translating what was being said. I was blessed with this coconut water over a series of chants, and then invited to drink the water that remained in the coconut. Almost instantly, the gremlin activity stopped. I returned to my resort abode.

I slept well and woke up with a slight unease, so I repeated the coconut blessing. My forehead felt calm again, so I decided to meditate in my coconut palm alcove on the grounds. As I entered my meditation that morning, I felt myself wrapped in a beautiful purple glow that was penetrating my cells. Bit by bit, my heart started pulsating out warm green clouds that mingled with the purple and I was in complete bliss, bathing in a feeling of total, complete unconditional love. I opened my eyes and had the desire to write in my journal for a while. I started writing words of wisdom. They were flowing straight up, opening my senses and guiding me to different aspects of life.

The following day, after the coconut blessing, I was drawn to go up on the deck overlooking the harvested rice terraces. I connected with the birds and the clouds, and again had an unstoppable desire to write in my journal. Profoundly sweet, yet deep words of wisdom flowed through me again and onto the pages of the book. My logical mind was like an observer, simply marveling at what was happening here. My heart felt open and my body experienced a sense of inner peace.

I called my Scandinavian friend Jakob, told him about the third eye experience and shared that I had started writing down the words of wisdom. His immediate response was, "Oh your third eye is opening. Well, you will have to leave London, you know. You won't be able to take it."

"What has London got to do with my third eye?" I asked.

He ignored my question and continued, "You will know it's open when your room lights up and there is an earthquake. Until then you are fine, enjoy the process."

"How do you know all this?" I asked,

"I just do, it happened to me a long time ago and I had to leave my country to feel in my center again," he said.

"Whatever... he is weird," I thought.

That night, after the third coconut blessing, I went to bed feeling both curious and blissed. At 3:00 am all the lights in the room switched on by themselves. I sat up, my heart racing, excited, thrilled and frightened all at the same time, wondering whether the earthquake would happen. Part of me wanted it and the other was just praying it did not happen. And then, there it was: the Earth shook, the bed rattled, a vase fell to the floor. We had an earthquake in Bali. The Earth stopped but I was still shaking all over, not knowing what to expect. After a time I switched off all the lights, snuggled into bed and closed my eyes really tight. The very next day I was to return to London.

Everything seemed normal. The gremlin activity had stopped completely and my world was cleaner, brighter, fresher and more fragrant. I was happy and ready to return home to London. I knew there were big decisions to be implemented when I got back. I was a little anxious about it and chose to release the anxiety, focusing instead on the amazing rebirth I had experienced during my three weeks here in paradise.

When I arrived at the airport, I realized my third eye was indeed open and that life was never going to be the same again. I was now able to see each person for who they truly are. I also knew instantly any incongruence they were in, the effect this had on their physical being and the conflicts it was causing in their relationships.

That day at the airport, I entered into the real world of absolute pure magnificence that each one of us embodies. I could also see the fractured human disguises that we all walk around with, believing that the human disguise is us. We start rejecting or getting trapped by, or trashing and fighting, these fractures. This results in even greater damage in the process. I wanted, I *so* wanted to help and reconnect each person to their inner beauty, their own divinity, to the magnificence they were born with. The problem felt huge and overwhelming. *"If this was the case in Bali, what would London be like?"* I wondered. Maybe, just maybe, my Scandinavian friend was right. *"I may want to leave London after all, who knows?"* As the plane took off I closed my eyes, asking my guides to show me the way.

New Beginning

I returned to London and chose to stay with my sister. I asked to meet Peter for lunch. When we met, I shared with him the dolphin meditation experience and my understanding that we were both ready to move on to the next phase of our lives. I requested that our relationship as a couple come to an end, and that a new beginning be allowed to emerge for each of us. Here we would each walk our path and celebrate all that has come about through our relationship with each other. I shared that I felt our relationship was fine and that nothing was wrong with it, except that it was now complete. I invited him to celebrate with me a new beginning for our separate lives going forward. His response was, "This is the first time you are asking for what you want, and I am happy about that."

We came together with our friends and family, to acknowledge a happy ending to our relationship and to celebrate a new beginning. Each person shared their gratitude for what we had meant to them as a couple and gave us their wishes and inspiration for the fresh start we were about to make.

It was such a HUGE shift in being for me. I would literally just burst into dance and started dancing every day, full of unleashed, unbridled joy. I started receiving amazing poetry that I called "downloads," and I began writing prolifically. I felt so connected to nature, the birds, the trees, the clouds, the sun and the moon. Evening after evening, I experienced the most spectacular sunsets London had ever seen. Every day was a fresh new start to another amazing experience. I walked, meditated, went chanting and even joined a law of attraction group. I was manifesting the kind of life experiences I had only dreamt about.

I understood that the law of vibration is the precursor to the law of attraction; I created my own games to keep my vibrations high and in tune. As I was becoming happier and happier, the world around me was transforming, too. There was lots of laughter and smiles at my sister's place. Sai and I were joyous, too, and I reconnected with my first husband after 18 years, to complete our relationship. Although this did not go quite as well as anticipated, I took it in my stride. I was still pleased I met him.

As I was becoming a more fluent receiver and transmitter of cosmic wisdom, I began to implement what I was writing, bringing my own life into congruence with the divine messages I was receiving. As a result of doing this, I got that my time in London was indeed complete. I decided to move away from London and take a year-long sabbatical in Bali. I arrived just before the volcanic ash from Iceland grounded all planes in and out of Europe.

Our Balinese friend Buana and his family took Jakob and me under their wing and introduced us to the spirit of Bali and the spirituality practices there. We would get dressed in temple attire and go to the different Balinese temples, often arriving just before midnight. Each time we got to a temple, by sheer coincidence we would find a priest and he would happily perform a ceremony and prayer for us. I would go into a deep meditation and emerge with yet another powerful download. I started writing and drawing the visions that were being given to me during these visits. Over the course of the next six months I visited 36 Balinese temples.

We experienced many magical and miraculous adventures; it was a taste of what was to become the norm in my life. I remember vividly the first time we went to the Elephant Cave temple. It was 11:00 pm, we arrived in the dark, it was so late that the priest and his family were already asleep. We quietly entered the cave, burned the incense and sat down on the floor to meditate. I felt so beautifully cocooned by the warmth of a protective bubble. The meditation was enlivening; we came out of it and noticed that at the opposite end of the entrance to the cave there was another entrance to somewhere. When we stood there, we heard the sound of fast-flowing water.

We decided to follow the sound of the water and this took us around behind the temple and down a long, steep flight of rough-cut steps. There was a river alright, and a small bridge made out of tree branches. On one side of the bridge was a HUGE Buddha head that had rolled down from the top of the mountain (during the volcanic eruption in the 1960s, I later discovered), and on the other side of the bridge was a HUGE tree with massive roots all around it, growing up out of the ground. The tree felt like a massive, saintly being and I was drawn to touch it and to be in the embrace of its roots. I knew then that this was a very special tree of life. It was filled with light orbs, which were dancing all around me. The communication I was receiving was grounding and exhilarating all at the same time. The big message was: *Know your roots and stay rooted; know that wherever you go, there you are.*

We continued walking up the hill. It was pitch dark and it was also new moon. We had a little light from a tiny Nokia phone. There was a thrilling, happy excitement in the air, as if I were on an Enid Blyton adventure trail. After walking past a cascade of waterfalls, we arrived at a stretch of rice fields. It was dark and we knew intuitively that there was a path to walk diagonally across, but where was it? It was not so visible in the dark. Then I remembered my third eye. We closed our eyes and the place lit up as if by a lamp; we saw the path (or rather felt the energy of it) and walked safely across to the other side. When we opened our eyes, we were in the middle of the temple compound. It took our breath away, filling our beings with complete gratitude and love for this new co-creation partnership with nature. I also remembered my foundation of always BE Learning. I had learned that day to apply the prowess of my third eye to serve a higher purpose and to this day I continue to apply it to facilitate that which is necessary for the highest good.

So...

BE Joy

Who or what are you going to let go of NOW to create space for what you truly desire?

Unconditionally accept what is, and this will allow you to open the floodgates of flow in every area of your life.

Are you ready to get set and go?

BE JOY to receive joy, enjoy and rejoice at the flow of joyous moments that become the norm in this journey of BEing JOY.

What life experiences have you had that you have shut out because you did not understand what was going on, or you were too shy to be seen, maybe as a freak?

How does it feel to embrace your innate wisdom, all of it, unconditionally, giving yourself the freedom to imagine what if... what if it were true?

CHAPTER 8:

BE AWAKE

Miracles Galore

The miracle bandwagon was cranking up and starting to get into gear. The story I'm guided to share is the time we traveled to visit Pasar Agung, the temple on the way to the highest volcano in Bali. This is the temple that is home to the Goddess of the Markets. We arrived at the temple, and this time the meditation produced an unusual visualization: it was of a corporation, with international offices and a tax structure that I know in the past I would have paid hundreds of thousands of dollars for. I knew then that this was a new business in the making. I was being shown what would become apparent to me once I was ready to emerge into the business world again.

We returned to the villa where we were staying. The ocean was loud and it was 2:00 am, so we decided to stand on the deck for a moment, looking at the waves that were being lit up by the lights from the villa. The breeze was serene; it felt amazing just receiving and accepting with grace all the blessings we had just received at the temple. I knew that a new doorway had opened and that I was being invited cosmically to cross the threshold. Just as we were quietly contemplating the happenings earlier at the temple and feeling at one with the ocean, we noticed the light beaming from the villa. It looked as if it was raining heavily.

We put our palms out and felt a few droplets and looked at each other, a little surprised and spooked. We decided to go to our separate rooms. I got to the entrance of my bedroom and sure enough there was a puddle of water in front of the door. It was raining all right. I had a red chiffon top on with a silk sarong, which was just moving gently with the breeze. I realized then that it had rained all around us and not on us, as if there had been an invisible umbrella held above our heads, shielding us, keeping us in the warm embrace of the goddess' blessings that we had just experienced. It was a miracle that made my heart sing.

I felt so blessed to be worthy of such a miracle. I called Ellen to check in about what had occurred. My guides explained that this night was the start of a powerful partnership of co-creation with the Universe and, in order for me to believe the scale of miracles that would be unfolding over the next stages of my life, the Universe had to show me one. It had to be done in such a way that it broke the pattern of shaping the future based on past experiences. Hence the miracle of "It didn't rain on us." I could not deny that it had occurred, and yet nothing from my past know-how could explain what had happened. I just accepted it as a gift.

This experience of "It didn't rain on me" has occurred on two further occasions: once during a storm in Perth and again in a river gorge, where I was asked to wait while the rest of my team went on to survey a potential piece of land. I was invited intuitively into a clearing in the forest, away from the gorge of a dry riverbed. I entered the clearing and found myself in a specially energized, perfectly ionized microclimate, where there was a soft gentle breeze. I was blessed with the revelation of my soul name, MARYEL. I felt so much joy in my heart and the trees around me celebrated by swaying and rustling their leaves.

I had just returned to the edge of the river gorge, beaming in the fresh energy of my soul name (blushing actually, my cheeks felt flushed), when a Balinese man with a big umbrella walked across this deep, dry river gorge and came up to me, and handed me the umbrella. I was perplexed. *"Why is he doing this?"* I was busily writing in my journal and did not understand why I required an umbrella. He tried to communicate with me and finally, looking dejected, gave up and left. He kept looking back at me as he was walking away, with a strange, surprised look on his face, until he went out of sight. I was receiving another outline for my new business in the making, so I kept writing in my journal until my friends arrived. They were all soaking wet, drenched; I walked with them to the car, still wondering why they were dripping so much. It was only when we sat in the car and the wipers had to be turned on that it dawned on me that it had rained all around me but not on me.

These experiences firmly set the foundation of BEing Trust and allowing the new paradigm wisdom to flow through me with ease and grace. I realized then that the gates in my miracle dam were now open. (Watch this space; the gushing is about to commence!)

Volcanic Ash and Breast Lump

Due to the volcanic ash, my flights were delayed, so I decided to visit Perth, Australia, the hometown of several of the new friends whom I had met in Bali, the gift-bearing angels. Sitting around one morning at the Fremantle market, my friend Kathy talked about a non-invasive breast examination that one of her friends did, and how helpful it had been for her in the early diagnosis of her tumor. There was really no reason for us to be having this conversation; it was quite a random input into the space. My friend Jakob asked her to book an appointment for him, as he was having a lingering pain in his right breast region. So she did.

As circumstances would have it, Jakob was unable to go to the appointment, so I went instead. This was an infrared, heat-sensitive diagnosis and they found a lump the size of a golf ball in my right breast, at the exact same spot where Jakob had been experiencing pain. They recommended that I see my doctor and get a mammogram. Well, I became concerned as I too could feel the lump. I decided to return to London and get it checked. I went through a series of tests and examinations. The lump was benign, but large enough to require being removed surgically.

I do not like medical interventions, and least of all surgical procedures. I meditated deeply, asking to see what I needed to see for this lump to have shown up at this stage in my journey. All I got was that it would be treated and at the right time I would be told how. I had my final pre-op appointment with a panel of medical doctors on the upcoming Monday, and all the final tests were completed on Friday. I did not want to go into surgery, so was anxious about how it could be averted. I chose to release the anxiousness. I decided: *I am a perfectly healthy person and my body is a master healer of its own ailments.*

I chose to BE Healthy, feel perfect and BE Joyous, celebrating that all was well on Monday. Every hour on the hour that weekend, I went on a rampage of appreciation and gratitude. I danced, did yoga, went for a walk in Regent's Park, and had a girls' evening out with my friends where we danced together. I knew we were celebrating another evolution and stepping across another threshold.

Monday morning arrived. I woke up early and on looking out the window at the amazing cloud formations from the eighth floor, I noticed a raven on the windowsill. Never had I seen a raven this high up before, so I knew it was a message for me. I was told: *"Now is the time for you to be healed and for the lump to be released. It is to be done using water and Jakob is to bring through and transmit healing energy, without any attachment or expectations. Let spirit do the work they wish to do."* I stayed in a quietly contemplative space. Jakob was in Perth, and it was late at night there. I relayed the message for him and let him do his thing, while I quietly returned to my joyous appreciation routine that I enjoyed so much.

At 6:00 pm I arrived at the clinic. The panel was formidable and my reports were lit up along the walls. The consultant who was to preside over my operation was the first to step forward and he said, "Before I walk you through what is going on and what has to be done, I would like to perform a physical examination."

"Sure," I replied, and returned to BEing Healthy in my mind, appreciating quietly.

He examined the breast, looked at my doctor and asked when the last mammogram had been taken; she told him it had been on Friday. He asked for another one to be done immediately, while they waited. I was sent to radiology and returned with my reports in hand. They put them up against the light. They were completely different. There was no lump; it was gone. The nurse and two other doctors examined my breast as well and shook their heads – there was no lump. The consultant said, "All we can say is that this can sometimes happen with tumors and cancers. You are one of the lucky ones. You can go home now and celebrate with your family."

I thanked them and left. Stepping out of the clinic, I jumped high, lifting my arms up in the air, and ran all the way to Regent's Park. I stood by the pond watching the swans and shed tears of complete joy. I felt free! It was a massive release from the shackles of physical disease and all the debilitating conversations around it.

I refused to relate to myself as a woman with a lump in her breast. Instead, I chose to BE Healthy, BE Appreciative and BE Happy that all was working out in my favor. And so it was.

Here was more evidence, delivered as a miracle by the Universe, right into my lap. It was a personal experience that could not be denied, and could not be explained. I just allowed myself to receive it, and I accepted the blessing. I received the message that **there is nothing to forgive, and nothing to forget; there is only to allow, receive and accept.**

I checked in with my guides through Ellen: What had happened there, what was I being shown? I was told that the lump had appeared as a symptom of not caring for myself over the years, having put everybody else's needs before my own. It had gotten worse as a result of my being disconnected from my purpose. It departed because I had gotten the message, though the energy signature of the tumor was still present.

For the next six weeks I was guided to consciously step onto my path and to allow spirit guidance to flow through me with ease, joy and grace.

I was to put ME first from now on, and then even the energy signature would go away, my guides said. I followed that guidance and have remained completely healthy, in my joy and in graceful appreciation of all there is.

Going Down Under with the Pelicans, Dolphins and Whales

Finally in June I moved to Australia, on my way to Bali. I had had the lump disappearing experience and I was now choosing ME and following my six pillars of living an extraordinary life every day. I felt confident that this change in lifestyle would release the health conditions that I had been diagnosed with, which included hypothyroidism, hormonal imbalance, type 2 diabetes and hypertension. I found a beautiful home overlooking the Swan River. I spent the mornings continuing my practice of pranayama, yoga, meditation and journaling. I would spend the day in my office above the river; my evenings were mostly with friends or talking to Peter on Skype, supporting him in his online dating.

I started receiving deep, powerful, amazing poetry and it would often be triggered by an unusual sighting of either a single dolphin or a school of them swimming in the river, or a flock of three pelicans or several geese, flying in perfectly choreographed formation in the sky. I started sharing my writings with my mother, whose health was deteriorating rapidly, as well as with my sisters. I was surprised and sometimes overcome with emotion, reading what had been transmitted to and through me. As I became even more in tune with my spirituality, I started to receive the wisdom in public places, too: at clubs, restaurants, and concerts. My visits to Bali continued every two to three months and each time I went, I would dive deeper and deeper into my true self. My spiritual growth and transformation was now very rapid and on a roll.

It was all beautiful and happy until one visit to Bali, when Jakob and I went to the Besakih Temple. It was midnight, as usual, and we felt the strong energy of this mother of all Bali temples. We were drawn to this particular spot to perform our own meditation and Jakob and I sat down facing each other, about three feet apart. In this meditation we both saw a silhouette of me with my head shaved. I was shocked and opened my eyes just when he opened his. He had this impish smile on his face and I knew instantly that he had also seen what I had been shown. I said, "You are the man; *you* are shaving your head, not me." He laughed wickedly and pulled a strand of hair from my crown, placing it on the altar as an acknowledgment of the instruction received. I thought nothing of it.

At the time I was engaged in being with my mother. She was choosing to cross over and, while in her comatose state, was communicating telepathically with me. I went to India. I was writing in Hindi and English as she crossed over and she described her experiences of moving to the new dimension. Upon her passing, I felt her presence, as well as her joy and relief at reaching and uniting with her twin soul.

Since I was in India, I went through a full eight-hour medical diagnostic to check all my health markers. I was confident that all was well, and it was. Thyroid perfect, glucose tolerance tests perfect, heart and blood pressure perfect, hormones balanced and cholesterol perfect, too. I was pleased and life cruised along nicely. I was living an extraordinary life with ease, grace and joy where all day was work and all day was play.

I returned to Perth. February arrived, and each day that I meditated, I saw the silhouette with my head shaved. Finally, on 8th March when the world was celebrating 100 years of International Women's Day, I chose to go to my usual hairdresser, Alan. I asked him to take it all off.

"Let's go really short, Mynoo," he said.

"No Alan, all of it has to come off today. Today is the day."

So he did it, and something very surprising happened. As the razor went over the last strip of hair on my head, I felt as if an entity of fear left my body. I felt like I had stretched out my arms and opened my wings for the very first time. I knew then that I had entered a brand new phase and stepped over another threshold.

The Monk on the Nudist Beach

With my bald head, my connection to cosmic wisdom became even more rapid. I was writing every day and living full out, releasing and letting go of all that did not serve me. My cells were feeling more and more exhilarated. I went on whale-watching tours, knowing for sure that lots of them would show up to greet me and be with us, doing their dance, displaying their gifts and communicating with me. I have received at least two amazing whale songs, rich in wisdom and insights. I also knew that we would have schools of dolphins come out to play. Surprisingly, three pelicans would show up, right on cue, just before my download would appear. I also loved the fact that I only had to drive out of town for half an hour and I was in the Australian outback, where I could connect with the Milky Way. I just lay on the hood of the car watching the sky for hours, enjoying the clusters of pearls and the clouds surrounding them.

Australia introduced me to the aliveness of life. You maneuvered your way around life and the many threats to it every day. It could be the redback spider or the brown snake or regular sightings of sharks in the water. I learned to embrace all life and understood that death indeed is a new beginning. I was now ready to receive my penultimate gift. I was guided to go into two weeks of silence, to connect, embrace and fully embody my unique gift to the world.

I had already done two silent weekends, in a retreat center outside Perth linked to a Buddhist monastery. So I decided to call them to see if I could do my own silence retreat there for two weeks. I was told it was an unusual request and that the head monk, Ajahn Brahm, would have to speak with me. I agreed and waited for his call, deciding to give him three days before I followed up with them again.

I was staying by the ocean, so every morning I would go for a walk on the beach. On the third day I proceeded with my regular walk. There had been shark sightings the day before, due to which the beach was unusually quiet, just a few early-morning fishers waiting for their baits to strike. I kept walking. I felt there was something special in the air that day, so I walked a long way. I suddenly saw a man walking toward me, in a loose white nightshirt, unbuttoned and displaying his package. I was shocked and turned around and just as I was doing so, I saw another man completely nude stretching out on the sand. I kept turning and a couple, completely nude, were putting up a tent. I finally turned around facing the other way, ready to start walking back, when a nude hunk winked at me just as my phone rang.

I was extremely shocked and uncomfortable. I answered the phone; it was Ajahn Brahm. I told him it was not the best time for us to speak and he said, "This is it." It was unusual for him to make this call, so now was my chance to discuss my personal silence retreat. I stopped, walked into the ocean and allowed the drama I was feeling to be released into the ocean. I explained the parameters for my use of the retreat center for two weeks to be in my own silence. He agreed and I was ecstatic, standing fully clothed on what I later discovered was a nudist stretch of the beach.

I drove to the retreat center with my Vitamix and an ample supply of organic fruit and veggies. This was a 93-acre estate and I had one of the units to myself. There was no one else staying there. All the monks lived in the monastery, which was a few minutes drive away. I also brought two empty journals. I knew this retreat was special so I was prepared. I met the caretaker and she explained that she would only be there for an hour or so every morning. Other than that, I was on my own. Well, I soon found out that I was not alone. The large estate was surrounded by the Australian bush so it was rich in many animal species, especially birds, as well as insects of the most unusual kind. I just asked the trees to envelop me in their OK-ness again, and invited the animal kingdom beings to come out and play as my mates.

I had the most amazing revelation of who I am, what is to occur and come about as a result of me being in my essence. I was to share my unique gift of love of self, and to leave people truly, madly, deeply in love with themselves. I spent hours and hours in the meditation halls. In the evening, at sunset, I would sit outside at the base of the pagoda with my mug of tea, watching the kangaroos, wallabies and emus run to their homes. Hundreds of magpies, parakeets and parrots were finding their resting places in the bush and a hive of activity was happening on the ground, with big red ants carrying their catches of the day to their anthills. The moon always showed up to light up the sky and show me the way to my home for the two weeks that shaped the design of what was to come next.

I wrote for hours — in the temple, in the bush and sitting at the base of the pagoda — feeling blessed, blissed and totally, truly, madly, deeply in love with me. I BEcame love and that love lit up my entire being. As we moved from the full moon to the new moon toward the end of my stay, my own light was bright enough to guide me to my home in the bush, that silent summer in Oz.

Kangaroo Coaching

After the silence retreat, I moved to live in the hills. My new home was on the top of the hill and belonged to a friend whose late husband, a German architect, had built it to be their private retreat. So for the three months that I chose to be there, it was like being on a breathtakingly beautiful holiday retreat with our own visiting family of wild kangaroos. The deck overlooked not just the rolling boulders of smooth elephant rocks as they cascaded down the hill, it also had the view of the ocean and the city in the distance. It was a huge 180-degree vista all around. The sunsets were spectacular and the rainstorms very often produced huge, full double rainbows.

There was a long driveway lit by solar lamps leading to the front of the house. One night, I arrived home after a long day, turned into the drive and was met by the deep red fluorescent sparkle of four eyes. Papa kangaroo and baby kangaroo were waiting at the end of the drive. They jumped along and followed the car and when I got to the end of the drive in front of the house I noticed 15 kangaroos just sitting there watching. I turned off my headlights and waited in the car, hoping they would go away. They did not. So I stepped out and gently entered the house, wondering what this experience was about. The next day I came home and again papa and baby greeted me at the end of the drive, escorted my car and joined the line of 15 kangaroos waiting for me. I stayed in the car longer this time, wondering if I was to receive a download from these majestic beings. No, nothing arrived. I gently opened the door, stepped out of the car and went inside the house.

The third day the same routine happened, except this time the whole family of papa, baby and mama with a joey in her pouch were there to greet me and joined the line of kangaroos waiting outside the house. I got out of the car this time and moved toward them, marveling at their neon-red retinas shinning at me. I said, "Tell me what you want me to know. I'm here."

We looked at each other silently and then their message arrived: **There is power in balance and when you get that, you can be powerful and still be balanced.** *You are strong, powerful and balanced, so if you ever feel threatened, just get into your stride and keep moving forward. Nobody has the audacity to keep going for you. You have the determination of being within you, regardless of what occurs around you. So keep moving, keep going and you will get there sooner than you realize. Anything you desire is only a hop, skip and a jump away.*

I thanked them for this wisdom and tears of joy and relief started running down my cold cheeks. As I wiped my tears away, one by one the kangaroos skipped away, out of sight into the dark hillside.

This advice from the roos came in handy sooner than I realized and continues to inspire me in a very practical way, even today. The 15 kangaroos did not return. Their job was done.

So...

BE Awake

Think about moments in your life when you were shown signs that you found interesting and chose to look past.

What is going on around you right now that carries a message or a reminder of something?

Is there an incident or a message or a person who keeps showing up in your space? What does that remind you of? Is there a message in this that will serve you in some way?

Is there a part of your life that you have compromised? Are you willing to BE AWAKE, look it straight in the eye and discern what messages it has for you that you are to act upon right NOW?

CHAPTER 9

BE PRESENT, BE REAL

The Hug Breakthrough

I chose to keep my head shaved until I received guidance to grow my hair again. I was comfortable being me, *au naturel*, no make-up, just me. I often went to this special place in Perth to watch the sunrise and on the way back would stop at a bakery that made fresh baguettes and croissants. As I was driving home one morning, belly full, basking in the warmth of the glorious sunrise, I noticed a banner advertising The Global Women's Summit, happening on that day. I stopped and decided to go in. I was welcomed, even though I did not have a registration.

At some point during the conference, the American lady who was the founder and CEO of this international women's network, put three questions to the audience and invited us to respond. I put myself forward, and as I was speaking on the microphone, I noticed that the American CEO fell asleep. I felt embarrassed, quickly completed my sentence and went back to my seat.

Lunch was a part of this conference, so when we broke off for lunch, I found to my surprise that the American lady made a direct bee-line for me. When she got to me she held my hand gently and said, "Please sit next to me over lunch, will you?" "Sure," I replied, wondering what it was about.

When I did sit next to her she turned to me and said, "You thought I fell asleep, didn't you?"

"You did," I replied.

"I did not. When you were speaking my guides took me into a trance and said: *she is the one you have been looking for in 132 countries. You are the one.* I would like for you to join me as President of the organization."

I could not believe what I was hearing. I agreed to meet her the next day. I was not ready to return to the business world yet. I was enjoying being a free spirit without the need to conform to any norms, though I was flattered and surprised. I guess she had to close her eyes for her guides to show her my business acumen, which was not obvious from my bald head and long brocade jacket from Afghanistan. I told her how I felt and thanked her for her interest. She did not accept this and over the next four weeks she kept in regular communication with me, asking me to try it out for three months. I finally agreed, and off I went to the United States.

I was now living and working in Utah, connecting with powerful, amazing women from around the world. Applying the principles of high performance to this particular business was a great way to integrate my spiritual evolution with the business world. I found that I had developed a laser-focused clarity. I knew what was necessary to turn this business around, to embark on a fresh growth cycle. The possibilities were endless; however, I also saw that there were two key impediments to success, and I decided to evaluate my continued working there based on whether these impediments could be removed.

I dove right in and gave it my all. The impediments started highlighting the cracks as we entered my third month there, during the preparations for the annual conference in Los Angeles.

I spoke at the conference and shared my journey, for the first time, with nearly 500 women. My sister had traveled there from London, curious to see who I had become and where I was going. At the end of my talk the whole room stood up in an echoing standing ovation; I felt a little embarrassed and grateful, too. When I got off the stage, more than 200 women left their seats and queued up to hug me, telling me that I had told *their* story.

They were in tears and in absolute gratitude for what I had shared. This went on for hours and I broke down myself. In my heart I knew I had experienced a huge shift. This time I felt whole, in perfect balance and harmony within myself. I had stepped over another threshold, so I could BE Present, BE Empathetic and BE Compassion.

It became clear at the event that this job was not mine to do. I was here to balance my over-masculine field with my feminine. The hugs from these beautiful women connected me to my own femininity in a way that had never occurred before. I was balanced, and felt powerful in this balance. Now I could embrace being powerful and still remain balanced. I made the choice to return to Bali, stopping on the way at Mount Shasta in Northern California to celebrate what spiritualists were calling Ascension Day: 11/11/11.

Twin Flame Pyramid to the Mission of My Soul

Mount Shasta was heaving with excitement. The energy there was very strong. I was in downtown Shasta with two of my friends from California. One of them now lived there; she had moved there because, she said, the mountain called. We had a wonderful meditation and enjoyed a thrilling drive through the snow-clad forest to Ascension Point. Due to the snow, there were very few people on the mountain. We had the best seats, the best views and the best connection with the mountain. (More on this part of the experience later.)

Another friend had strongly recommended that we book ourselves in to meditate in the pyramid at Shasta, which had been built by a twin flame couple. When we arrived and saw the pyramid, I was aware of its power and became anxious about feeling claustrophobic inside.

The owner assured me that if I just tapped the entrance door he would immediately come over and open it so that we could exit.

I need not have worried; when I stepped into my meditation I was swept into an extraordinary experience where I saw elaborately dressed goddesses, archangels, angels, celestial beings and masters. It felt as if they were present to me, each in their majestic regalia. They were evidently communicating to me. I felt them becoming embodied within me, so that they could communicate through me.

After the initial energetic activity calmed down, I entered a realm of complete silence and stillness. A purple hue engulfed me again and I was given the message that I was to go to Bali to meet Jakob where we would be blessed with the initiation of our soul. After the initiation we were to receive the mission of our one soul. I was introduced to many masters, goddesses and archangels who would bear witness to this divine energetic experience in Bali.

From that day onward, every time I meditated, these energies that I later understood as Ascended Masters, metaphysical energies, would appear. I would receive their names, most of which I did not recognize. I would write them down and search them on Google afterwards. At least I knew they were serious when the names were Archangel Michael or Archangel Raphael and so on. Each of them would share a message with me, which often contained a nugget of profound wisdom.

Initially, I questioned what was happening to me. Then I realized that it was a divine blessing of wisdom that I was receiving. I did not hear voices or sounds and often did not see anything, either; I just had a knowing and wrote down what was being sent out through me. Once I chose to simply receive without questioning what was happening, the flow became smoother and even more powerful, and I started rejoicing in the miracles that started unfolding as a result. This level of comfort was necessary to prepare me for what was to occur next. I request that you too set aside your apprehensions and receive the nuggets and insights from what I am sharing here.

I returned to Bali as guided. Jakob arrived a few days later and we got into a car with our usual driver. I was still bald and Jakob decided to shave his head too. We told our driver that we would be guided, so he should just follow our instructions and we would be brought to the perfect place. He was a bit nervous but agreed to go on this adventure with us. After four hours of guided driving we were asked to go down an alleyway and to stay there for the night. We were asked to let our driver return to be with his family, four hours away.

We were at a small resort on the ocean in the north of Bali. We checked in and were guided to create a holy mandala and sit opposite each other with the mandala and the altar on a small table between us. We lit the candles and closed our eyes. I did not know what to expect; I had never done this before and chose to just BE Present, BE in the moment and BE in flow.

A scene like a court of a palace came into our vision and the Ascended Masters who had agreed to bear witness started gathering all around us. We first received a beautiful blessing and a helix encased in a purple column, emerged from our being as the energy field of our soul initiation.

Mary Magdalene stepped forward and placed a light in my heart.

Mother Mary put her right hand on my left shoulder and gave us the mission of our one soul, "It is to expect and accept miracles and have that become the norm."

Lord Shiva continued, "This to be rolled out through Palaces of Extraordinary Miracles."

Mother Gaia, Goddess Parvati and Goddess Lakshmi joined in, "Where nothing leaves the palace, except enlightened, awakened human beings and fresh, free-flowing drinking water."

Archangel Michael stepped forward and joined with Lord Vishnu and St. Germain, "When you are called to do the work and you step up, all obstacles are gone, taken away. All the resources, people and opportunities you require will land in your lap."

St. Germain continued, "Your soul action is to challenge the status quo, and you will start with relationships."

We were then taken on a flight in the purple column of St. Germain, with eagles on our right and condors on our left. We were shown visions of what would be going on in the world, with the Palaces of Extraordinary Miracles in operation and the new way of life, expecting and accepting miracles as being the norm. We were taken to different dimensions too, to see what effect this vibration emanating from this planet had on our galaxy and other star systems. Four hours and 49 minutes later we emerged from this meditation, flying high in complete silence and still in awe of what had just taken place.

I was drawn to go toward the ocean; the sun was starting to set and a fisherman had just anchored his fishing boat. I asked if he would take me into the water. He did not understand English, but the energy of my request was clear. He helped me get into the boat and we sailed into the sea. I closed my eyes; the vision flight with the eagles and condors had left me feeling chilly. The warmth of the sun on my eyes and skin felt good. The hum of the engine was comforting and I felt like I had entered the womb again with the cradling of the boat by the ocean. This continued for a while and then, with no warning, the engine stopped and the boat started circling. I heard the fisherman saying something excitedly in his language I could not understand, so I just stayed in the flow of what was occurring, knowing that all was well. I had my hands on my heart and was breathing in love, kindness and compassion. And that's when I saw it.

There it was, right in front of me. My every cell lit up, my heart opened and my mind just relaxed as we entered Dolphin City. There were just over 54 dolphins of all ages. A few were leaping and circling the boat in a playful way; some were displaying their joy in front of us and several were grooming each other. I just joined my palms in a *namaste*.

They had all come out in acknowledgment of what had just been given to us. They were here to let me know that we were still connected. *Call on us if you require clarity, and don't forget to play.* I also received a strange command from the dolphins: I was now to step into a whole new aura. As my new personality was emerging, their message to me was: *BE prepared. You will look, feel, and even BE You, so your appearance will change beyond what you can imagine now.* I was curious.

The sun had set by now, so we started the engine; the dolphins dispersed and we returned to the hotel. I felt totally satisfied and fulfilled. A few days later the acronym PoEM (for Palace of Extraordinary Miracles) arrived, and from that point on, it became the reason for coming alive in the moment and living moment by moment.

So...

BE Present BE Real

What brings you alive? What gives you a surge of vitality?
What does it feel like, experiencing that surge of being alive?
Where in your body do you feel it? When you are engaged
in what your calling is, you feel absolutely alive. When you
are present and grounded in reality, you come alive.

To achieve this, practice the art of acute observation of what
is right there in front of you, in you and around you. Rejoice in
the wonders that all these things embody, and share them.

PART THREE:

THE BIG FAT INDIAN WEDDING

In this section I share the rather stark reality of what it took for me to embrace the courage required for my journey of awakening. It is all about being authentic and true to ourselves, and anything that is not congruent with that will be right in our face. (And for me, it was literally in my face!)

At this point in my life I thought I was already whole and complete. I'd had business and real world experiences. I'd had spiritual awakenings and felt my connectedness with my own spirit, the spirit of nature and our spirit guides. I knew how to incorporate the esoteric into my day-to-day living. I knew how to share my experiences and to speak about them without alienating people.

I thought I was now ready to cruise when I suddenly received a whole new gift: very deep and permanent healing ability. I became a spiritual physiological surgeon, guided to address the root cause of physical discomforts and ailments by releasing and removing the energetics of emotional stress and trauma. Until this new ability began to take hold, I thought I knew everything at that point. Fortunately, I had learned to unconditionally accept what is, so I was able to receive and accept what was being gifted to me and apply it to support and rejuvenate traumatic and chronic distress situations.

(Once again, I invite you to stay on the journey with me and receive the nuggets that are relevant for you, without getting distracted by your logical brain trying to make sense of it all. I share this as the most effective strategy that continues to serve me. It lifts me to greater and greater levels of spiritual evolution and practical implementation.)

CHAPTER 10:

BE TRUST

Surrendering My Will

My journey into the silent world of tapping into cosmic wisdom had begun. I started receiving regular guidance in my meditations to go into periods of silence. These periods ranged from 36 hours to three days. Each time, I was given a focus topic for the silence.

During the period of silence, Ascended Masters and celestial energies would gather around me, in the form of the court of a palace; each one stepped forward and gave me their wisdom on the topic I was working with. Quite often I also received step-by-step processes, so that I could implement the wisdom with which I had just been blessed.

It was after one of my three-day periods of silence, where the focus was on love and creating a new communication with love, that I received this message:

> *We invite you to surrender your will to the will of the All-Knowing, knowing that the All-Knowing knows best. All obstacles are gone, taken away and you emerge deeper and higher into your true self, walking your path and realizing the mission of your soul.*

At first I was shocked: *Surrender my will?* In typical rebel fashion, I resisted the idea of relinquishing the control I thought I had over my life. I checked in with Ellen, and she explained that 12 years earlier, she too had been asked to do the very same thing. She shared that her experience was that all her needs really *were* taken care of. She was able to accomplish all that was required of her as well as to live in the "real world," being certain and confident. She suggested that I ask my guides to show me what this would mean, and to allow them to do this over the next 60 minutes. After that I would *have* to choose.

I did that, and was taken on another extraordinary tour of all the aspects of my life and what I was to cause in the world. I wrote it all down. It was an exquisite, amazing experience with fresh challenges and new opportunities, and I was implementing all that I am here to do with crystal clarity. There were uplifting, loving transformations that were being birthed as a result of my surrender to the All-Knowing. I returned from the 60-minute ride feeling complete and serene. I accepted the request. **I chose to BE trust, and plugged into my inner knowing.**

One day I was in an early morning breakfast meeting and I was guided to ask our architect, who was smoking, for a cigarette. I did this despite never having smoked before. Naturally, as I inhaled, I started coughing. Everybody was a little shocked at what was happening there, so no one said anything. I was guided to take three inhales and stop. My coughing spells were strong and severe. When I stopped, I realized that the constant tickle I had had in my throat was gone. This was a condition with which I had suffered since I was 19 years old. People often said they knew I was around because of this niggling cough I had. And now, it was gone.

I was surprised and relieved to know that I do indeed have another layer of supporters looking out for me in a very real way. It boosted my trust and my confidence that all is well and occurring in perfect timing and perfect order. I only had to BE Trust.

That same evening, I was guided to go to the open mike gathering at a local cafe and, just as we were leaving, I was asked to pick up and take my blue book with me. When we entered the cafe, the list to jot your name down for the act you wanted to perform was right at the entrance. I was guided to put my name down and to write "Surprise" in the column for the act I was going to share. I stayed in trust and joined my friends in enjoying the music, the singing and the comedy when the organizer said, "So now let's have a surprise... please welcome: Mynoo."

I stood up, feeling instant panic. *"OMG, what now?"* There were over 200 people in the cafe. A few were seated, but most were standing. I was again guided to take my blue book with me.

I went to the front, sat on the performer's stool and just looked at the audience, waiting to receive the next set of instructions. They arrived, just in time. *Get people to raise their hands and pick three people.*

I finally spoke. "I am being guided to share a gift with just three of you, raise your hands if you are interested, curious or intrigued." Almost all the hands went up and I chose three in three different parts of the room. I was guided to flick through the pages of my blue book, asking each person to say "Stop" when they were guided to; I was to read to them what was written on that page.

The blue book was my journal, so it contained much received wisdom as well as personal insights and nuggets. Each person stopped at a different page. I read out the writing for them and each time I did, it touched them so deeply that they started crying in gratitude. It was as if they had received an answer to a long, deep question they had been seeking, and today I had gifted it to them from my blue book.

I was moved. It reinforced my new commitment to BE Trust.

What followed my time on the stage was interesting too. Several of the performers acknowledged what they had received from my readings for themselves, and came to thank me for sharing this divine wisdom with them. The tempo in the cafe became one of serene, graceful gratitude, as one by one people stepped into their inner truth. It was a major shift from the validation-seeking, vanity-infused atmosphere we had walked into earlier. Granted, there was a sense of fun in both environments; one was fun as it gave instant gratification and the other was fun as it left us feeling fulfilled in a deeper way.

I got to see that by me choosing to BE Trust, I became trusting of myself and released multiple heavy cloaks that had been held together by the thread of ego. I saw that BEing Trust meant that I was embodying the vibration of trust and was therefore attracting more to be trusting about. I learned to BE in the vibration, rather than to be about the business of doing, which would take me into the vibration of questioning or hoping that I could be trusting.

I was beginning to step over yet another threshold.

The Rainbow Brotherhood

I was returning to Bali after a business meeting in Jakarta. On the flight I decided to meditate and fill my heart and the entire airplane with the vibrations of love, kindness and compassion. It started off nicely and I was in my blissful light, which changed from gold to white to rainbow colors. At that point, I entered into a deep, trance-like state and I remained there until it was time to land. My driver was there waiting to pick me up and we were to go straight to a meeting with our architect. On the way, I received clear guidance to connect spiritually to a new group of celestial beings, who were calling themselves the Rainbow Brotherhood. They were coming onto the planet just then, bringing their vibrations to spread the energy of love that lasts. They were also to work with me to perform an energy surgery on my youngest sister, whom I knew had just gone into the hospital for treatment of fibroids in her uterus.

I cancelled the meeting with our architect and told the driver not to disturb me as I was going to be meditating in the car. I started the meditation and found that my sister was in severe pain, with a high temperature and a quickly-dropping blood count. I also saw tears rolling down her cheeks. Her eyes were closed. I felt a strong presence of my parents' energies. I noticed that my mother was showering champaka and jasmine flowers on her and my father was sitting at her feet. Mom was silent and just lovingly blessing her with the flowers. Dad (who had also crossed over, two months prior) on the other hand, was telling my sister, *"Look, where I am there is no pain, just come to me and all the pain will be gone."* The next thing the Rainbow Brotherhood guided me to do was to ask my father lovingly to step aside and allow us to take a chance at healing my sister. I made the request of Dad telepathically and he nodded and stepped aside, still present and watching.

I was guided like a moving x-ray machine to see what was occurring within her body. We found several lesions that were dripping blood, which explained the reducing blood count. We then entered the area that had been operated on. It was like entering a war zone. There was rampant destruction that seemed to have been caused by two dragon-teeth-like instruments. I realized then that they hadn't just removed the fibroids but had in fact removed her whole uterus. There was a pool of blood there, with an energy signature of fear and remorse. The cells in that entire region appeared severely traumatized. I was guided by the Rainbow Brotherhood to gently release the toxins and with the help of Mother Gaia we brought in the warm, soft, glowing, healing energy light, from the belly of the Earth.

We were guided to every cell in that region and we released the pain energy by dropping it into the core of the Earth. We filled every cell with love, kindness and compassion, shining the healing golden light into each one. Once the toxic energies and toxins were released, we bathed each cell in the rainbow energy of love that lasts and stayed there until all traumatic memories were released from every cell.

At last the whole region felt healthy, calm and at peace. I continued to meditate, slowly filled my sister's entire being with rainbow light energy and, when guided to, I returned to consciousness. My palms were hot, as if a jolt of life force had passed through them. The whole surgery to release the cellular memories had taken four hours and twenty-seven minutes.

Within three minutes of completing this surgery, I received a call from my middle sister, who was in India at the hospital with the younger one. She explained to me what had happened, not realizing that I already knew most of what she was telling me. I shared with her what had just occurred and she confirmed that our sister's temperature had just returned to normal and she had stopped crying, as the pain had suddenly reduced. The next day her blood count started going up again and within three weeks she was completely fit and healthy, back to normal and ready to join the Indian wedding of the decade, a few weeks later when our niece was married. People who were aware of her experience remarked that they could not believe she was so fit and active, given that she had just had a complete hysterectomy.

I later viewed the DVD she was given of her operation and witnessed the metal dragon-toothed machine doing its massacre. I understood how crucial it is to support any surgery with a cellular trauma release process for complete recovery.

My guidance from the Rainbow Brotherhood was to **BE Health and I will become healthy in all facets and aspects of my life.**

The Rainbow Brotherhood have performed many other physical, emotional and business surgeries, each time connecting the person or people to their true selves. I was also guided to launch a by-invitation-only energy surgery online. Since then, I have conducted several hundred of these procedures. They have been very effective and clarifying. I was so grateful for all these magical connections.

Turnip Face

Finally, we get to the month of the big fat Indian wedding. My eldest niece was getting married. This was the first wedding of this generation in our family, and it had been in the making for four years. We were all set, a whole new wardrobe had been put together for all the immediate family members, and we were all excitedly preparing to travel. My best friend arrived in Bali to spend some rest and rejuvenation time there. I had been traveling to and from Jakarta, getting everything lined up before I went away for the wedding. Two days to go before we left and we finally had some time to chat as friends. It was suggested that I get my hair colored to cover the gray.

Since I started growing my hair back, I had not used any products on it and even though the hair initially grew out completely gray, over time it had changed and become a nice salt-pepper color. I agreed to use the all-natural henna and natural indigo to color it, and voilà, my hair looked fantastic. We held a women's gathering in Bali at our home, and I even had a swim in the pool. I looked great, felt wonderful and was glad to have a fabulous connection with my women friends. We then organized the house so we could leave for the wedding.

The next morning, I woke up with a dull pain in my face. My eyes and earlobes were itchy. I looked in the mirror and was shocked: my face had swollen up to twice its normal size. My eyes were thin slits and my nostrils were flared, like the face of a very chubby baby. I reached out to my friends; we cut up aloe vera and applied it to my face, which felt flaming hot. I just didn't understand. What had happened? Was it the henna? Chlorine in the pool? What could have caused this?

"A negative energy attack," said Ellen. My guides supported me through a process to release some dark negative energy and my face calmed down and felt cool. The swelling subsided and by the time I was to leave for the airport, my face had shrunk back down, almost to normal again. However, it had become covered in fine lines and wrinkles. It was as though I had aged at least 20 years within just a few hours. The pain was gone, and my eyes had cleared up. The itchiness in my earlobes persisted, but at least I was able to travel, even if I looked like an old woman.

We arrived at the wedding home and everyone was at first excited to see me and then shocked at the condition of my face. Hospital appointments were booked but I put my foot down. I declared that I was going to allow my body to process this attack with healing light and meditations. I was to receive what was being shown to me through this process and to neutralize this condition. I also felt that I might be detoxing sugar. Two months earlier I had stopped having sugar of any kind. So rather than adding additional toxins to address the situation, I was going to let the toxins drain out, and allow my body to heal from within. (I also suspected that the sugar withdrawal might have triggered a release of fungus or even parasites.)

My family, however reluctantly, finally accepted my decision and left me to recover in my own way in my room. I would come out to join the rest of the family for our choreographed dance practices for the sangeet, a wedding ceremony solely dedicated to singing and dancing, and also for the delicious meals. I was so loving all the dancing and enjoying catching up with family, when I received guidance to have 36 hours of silence in the middle of it all. I then entered the zone of silence wisdom, which was focused this time on the theme of beauty and truth.

The following day, I woke up to my face looking as though it had been burned, as well as black and blue. My eyes had flared up again and were oozing a sticky liquid. The wedding was now only four days away and I was looking and feeling worse than I did when I had arrived.

Was I going through some kind of a strange facelift and face peel? As I worked with the Ascended Masters guiding me through beauty and truth, sharing their amazing wisdom, I started putting into practice what I was receiving. Cleopatra and Queen Sheba were among the ones gathered to support this silence. Cleopatra gave me a collection of recipes for face, hair, and body beautification products and Queen Sheba gave me exercises and solutions to enhance the sparkle in my eyes.

I started using the recipes and the eye exercises. My sister gave me an ultimatum, saying if my face did not return to its normal complexion within two days, I would have to go to the doctor and resort to steroid-based solutions. I asked my guides for help and within two days my skin tone cleared, but my face was still tender and swollen. "Turnip face" became my code name at the wedding.

Along with the energies of Archangels Raphael, Gabriel and Michael, I was guided by the Rainbow Brotherhood. Together we started the process of working though my digestive tract, section by section, releasing that which did not serve me and filling the cells with a beautiful healing light. All was well until we got to the small intestine.

Paradise to a Parasite

I could feel life within life, in fact clusters of lives within my being. The impression I received was of the mouths of little baby birds in a nest, waiting for the mother bird to arrive to feed them. I was traveling through the villi of the small intestine working inch by inch. There were several deformities that I came across; some I was able to correct, while others were left behind. I felt as though I was being sucked by a suction pump to get to the end. When I did get to the end, where the small intestine joins the colon, I entered what can only be called a living nightmare. I found clusters of parasites, and one large mother parasite in the colon. There were little floating creatures being birthed and released into the bloodstream too, infesting a few of my organs.

I was absolutely horrified, and had to be shut out by the metaphysical team that was working with me, so that they could do the major parasite clearing. I was then guided to ask the parasites to leave my body, and to give permission to my cells to rejuvenate and heal themselves. I asked the souls of the parasites to be released into the light. Archangel Michael dealt with the stubborn ones; the others were gently taken away by the Rainbow Brotherhood. As they worked, I could feel my insides becoming lighter and cleaner. Finally there was only one big one left, the mother parasite. This one would almost leave and then return into its body within my body. It all sounds so strange, and in my logical, left brain-dominated earlier self I would never have believed all this. It did happen in me, though, so I have first-hand experience of what it felt like.

Day 1 of the three-day Indian wedding celebration was now the next day. It was the day we had the song and dance show, where the two sides of the wedding party were to put on their best performances. The whole house and all the guests had their own dance routines and were being trained by our master choreographers, the bride-to-be and her sister. They were relentless in their drive for perfection. And there was I, coming out of the bedroom to practice my dance routines, then returning to work with the mama parasite again.

Finally I was to have a direct communication with this big mama. I asked what it wanted to share with me. I also explained to it telepathically that it had to leave. "Go you must, that time has come; so what are you waiting for?"

The creature telepathically replied that my body was its home. It had arrived there when it was little and I was little and we have grown up together. It has birthed many generations of offspring in my terrain and many of those have come and gone and it has managed to survive. It felt that it was in a partnership with me. Now it had to leave and it was afraid of what would be next. I asked it to go into the light, to follow the track of light laid out by Archangel Michael, and a new home for its soul in a different incarnation would be found. It was best that it chose to go by itself rather than be forced out, which would not have served either it or me. After 25 minutes of constant telepathic dialogue, to and fro, it finally released its soul to the track of divine light laid out by Archangel Michael.

A heaviness from my solar plexus lifted and I felt released. It was a different sense of freedom. I came out of my room looking and feeling radiant. There was a banquet laid out, filled with the most yummy delicacies from different parts of India. I had a small bowl and felt satisfied. I realized then that I had absolutely no craving for sweets or rice, the two weaknesses where, in the past, I had nearly always struggled with portion control. I had stopped having sugar and had to use a great amount of willpower to refrain from having it. This time, however, after the release of the big mama, I had no desire for sugar at all. No willpower was needed. It was then that I understood that the cravings had in fact been those of the creature that had taken up residence inside me. Now I was indeed free to be myself, feeding and nourishing *me* for a change.

When I received this understanding I also received intuitive guidance to embark on another silence, this time focusing on true love and romance. It felt like quite an inconvenience for me to be silent when the house was filling up with the wedding guests and the henna party was about to begin. My guides assured me that it was necessary for the wedding that we have our time on the subject of true love and romance.

After the henna applications, and singing and dancing to naughty wedding folklore songs, I returned to my room. It had been a huge day of massive release and reclaiming my space and identity. I knew that the carcass of the creature was still within me and would take several weeks, maybe months, to leave my physical body. I had to protect myself from the toxicity of the degenerating carcass. I went straight into a deep meditation. It was going to be an all-nighter of meditation and writing about true love and romance.

I sent the soft gentle healing rainbow light into my physiological systems and organs and asked my metaphysical healers to do their part in protecting and healing me as my body processed and discarded that which did not serve me. I was grateful to feel the vibrant vitality I had been missing for quite a while.

Day 1 of the wedding was here. We had over 1800 guests. The big glamorous sangeet, the song and dance show, was happening that night. My complexion was normal, though my face was still tender; so I looked like I was in pain but felt like I was 10 years younger. I had received a huge blessing of wisdom from the Ascended Masters overnight. I learned that there is nothing true or untrue about love. We as human beings *are* love. Romance is a way of living our life: having joy, a sense of adventure, smiling, laughing, sharing our experiences with people, being love. I made the choice: **I am to BE Love, BE Beauty and BE Romance. In making this choice I embraced all of the fractures impacting my human disguise and stepped in, plugged in and connected to the love, beauty and romance within me.**

This shift in my being introduced a sense of fun and a celebration of joy that I was experiencing in each moment. As a result, it gave permission for all to be comfortable around me and just join in the unbridled fun that followed over the next three days. The dance show was great. I did my party piece and enjoyed every moment of being in the spotlight. Every minute at the three-day, big fat Indian wedding was flawless, magical and filled with joy.

I understood the difference between **BE Beautiful vs. BE Beauty, where I own, embrace and embody the beauty within, so that it emerges and makes me beautiful in the eyes of the beholders.**

I understood the difference between **BE Romantic vs. BE Romance, where I embody the aliveness, sense of adventure and play in my cells and people around me cannot help but join in the fun.**

I understood the difference between **BE Loving vs. BE Love, where I am the essence of being human and this magnetizes a huge influx of love toward me, as I connect each person I meet to the truth of who they are at the core of being human: Love.**

I understood that when I become congruent with who I am on the inside, the outside steps in and multiplies many times over that which I have established within myself. So as I embody the beauty that I am inside of me, the outside responds by reacting, acknowledging and complimenting me on how beautiful I look. At the wedding, when focusing only physically, I actually looked a bit ill. Yet I received so many compliments. I believe what was happening there was that people felt me as beautiful, because I was in the state of beauty within myself.

So...

BE Beauty

I invite you to look at yourself in minute detail and find those aspects of you that you feel are beautiful. Acknowledge yourself for these and embrace these aspects of you. Then see this beauty spreading across your entire body, and experience being filled up by the beauty that is uniquely yours. Take five deep breaths and notice how beautiful you are. Step into your energetic beauty shoes and walk your path. Recognize and compliment yourself for the fullness of the beauty you now embody.

BE Romance

List a collection of things, writings, places, people, nuances and experiences that you have had that make you smile, laugh out loud and feel exhilarated. Every day, make a conscious choice to include at least one of these in your day and start living the romance way of coming alive. Share this joy with your friends. Go on a rampage of feeling and journaling that happy feeling. Allow yourself to feel romantic. Surprises will surprise you; write those down, too. This is your romance reality check; romantic interludes will follow.

CHAPTER 11:

BE LOVE AND BELOVED

The Date with God

We were all gathered in the church for what we called The White Wedding. My niece and her husband were looking beautiful and in love. It was a Syrian church, the choir singers were melodious and making all our hearts melt with the sweetness in their voices and the flow of the words. I was dressed in a yellow embroidered kaftan, the bride's mother and her sisters were dressed in yellow or gold accompanying the bride in white, with her bridesmaids in peach. It was a lovely, elegant blend of colors, with the flowers and decor to go with it.

I was sitting in the front row feeling beautiful, energized and vibrant when the priest stepped up to the podium. The music stopped and he began to speak his wise words and blessings for the couple, as they prepared to take their vows. I was feeling a huge sensation of love in my heart and it started to spread across my being. I was compelled to close my eyes and then I felt it.

My cells started to tingle with delight and I had a beautiful feeling of sunrise in every cell as it calibrated to perfect vibration. I was lighting up from the inside. I knew and felt: *It is the energy of God.* I had experienced it once before, and I knew from that previous experience that it uplifted my presence so powerfully that it could even disrupt the ceremony in progress. The priest had already become distracted, and had repeated his last two sentences three times; I knew he did not intend to do so again. So I stepped out of the church and allowed the message from God to be received in grace.

I started writing on my iPhone and with every sentence I stepped further and further away from the pretentiousness of what we call "love." I was dropping into the depths of my soul *being* love. The message I was receiving was for the couple and for each one of us. I knew then that a new commandment from which to live my life was being revealed to me. This message from God was a step in that direction.

Here is the message:

Word of God

> *Go easy, be light, let go of the seriousness you have given to my intentions. Be playful and innocent, live out the life you have been gifted. It's meant to be easy. So just chill out. Back up. Enjoy it.*
>
> *"The source of marriage is love," says the priest.*
>
> *"It is not," says God. "It's control."*
>
> *"It's dangerous to use the word 'love,'" says the priest.*
>
> *God reminds us:*
>
> *Love is you; it's you who is love. God sees you as love. Love is not IN anything, LOVE IS YOU. This is who you are.*
>
> *Life is about being love in its simplest form; that is what this human form is for. Live it full-out and deep within. Come alive being love.*
>
> *It's your choice. Make this choice for you. You are the only one that counts: all else is a distraction.*
>
> *You focus on being love coming alive as such and all your loved ones feel the shift and welcome you. Thank you for this.*

And even if they don't, their higher selves are rejoicing with you as they connect, bit by bit, to their beings being love. You come alive together and set your world alight with the beautiful, infectious experience of love that lasts.

Today you come together as two parts of one soul to fulfill your pact to spread your soul connection. Imbue it with the love that you are. Then experience each moment, rejoicing, celebrating this union of love. Enjoy the oneness that arises, and prepare to be surprised by the surprises that are now being drawn to you.

Receive them with open hearts and give your mind some rest, at least for a while. Three months or so will suffice and you will be one with who you truly are.

That is a promise. And since God delivers while man plans, how about we do this together this time? Come on, jump onto the ship and be one with me.

I welcome you. You are my tribe, it is so and so it is.

You are already blessed, you are already a part of my divine plan. You are now ready to embrace fully the divinity you embody, so come forth, take it on and multiply.

(The message continued in the royal "We":)

We love you, we adore you, we love you for who you are, have been and are becoming. We love you no matter what. We invite you to love you, to step into your divinity and to spread your unique blend of divine grace around. The world is waiting, ready and rejoicing for you.

Celebrate this moment and the moments that follow. Emerge in the moment. Go for it: live, love, laugh; abide in your own tranquility in the moment. Enjoy. Bliss out and shine your unique light. Thank you, thank you, thank you.

via Mynoo Maryel

I get it: when I can BE Love, I can BE Loved, I become the BELOVED and can be the beloved. It's a chain reaction of the sweetest kind.

I stopped seeking love and validation outside of me, and entered the realm of being whole and complete within myself. This in turn made me a magnet, drawing and attracting the love that matches my own frequency of love. This love is whole and complete, too, so we become partners in co-creating our life together, coming alive together without the neediness or stickiness of co-dependence.

Peeling Off Layers... A Metaphor

With this realization, it was time to shed the layers and layers of programing and conditioning that I had received, that each of us receives through our own beliefs and societal norms.

My body responded by matching the process I was going through spiritually. The wedding was over and my face returned to looking burnt, black and blue... only this time, the skin started peeling off. Every day it was as if a new layer was being peeled away. It was painful and looked painful. As layer after layer was removed, I began feeling lighter and lighter, both in my weight and also in the illumination my being was starting to embody. A few of us decided to celebrate the New Year at Auroville in Pondicherry, an entire city that had been received as a download to a divine mother and was sacredly built by her followers, even long after she had crossed over to the other dimension.

We were at Auroville, standing under one of the world's largest banyan trees, when I recalled a day when I was drawn to witness a spectacular sunrise. My own mother had been keen to communicate with me, soon after her crossing over. She had asked what I wanted to know and I was reminded of the questions I had asked and the answers I had received. They arrived again, right there under the banyan tree:

What is life?

Life is a physical state where the organism is breathing.
But it's the LIVING that really matters.
If you are not living then you are not alive.

What is death?

It is the opposite of life.
It is a shift in the physical state when the organism stops breathing.
It is a permanent shift that occurs in the moment.
One moment there is life, and in another moment it's gone... just like that!
But this too does not matter.
The degree to which you lived your life does.
You continue to live, inspire, impact and lead your tribe, long after you
have stopped breathing.
In many instances, this change of state creates an even greater swell in
the wave of the impact you can have on the planet.
Your sphere of influence grows and grows, beyond your wildest dreams.
All of this is a direct co-relation to you LIVING your life.

What is Love?

Love is who you are.
YOU ARE LOVE.
It is not what you get or what you give.
It is not about being in love or loving somebody, something, someday, one
day in the past, present or future.
You ARE love.
Love manifests when you are being love.
There is no true love or false love.
It just IS and... it is YOU.

This was profound, I was grateful to receive this reminder, a big reveal after the big peel. This time the New Year (k)new me and I re-emerged with baby-soft skin and sparkly eyes. I knew and understood that the **BE is about being in the vibration, not doing. BE in the vibe of the vibration of love and you become it, you manifest and magnetize it, in all different forms, in all aspects of your life.**

I got it. It is all about the BE. With this revelation the BE was born and I stepped into my glorious magnificence, being love.

I can choose to "do hard work" and "survive" and I will be a victim, reacting to the trials and tribulations of life; or I can choose to thrive and BE Extraordinary.

I choose to BE Alive and BE Love. Then I have love, health and vibrant vitality.

So...

BE Love

If you are seeking love, then go within yourself and distill all that you love about yourself. You can start with whatever you are most comfortable with and work your way through all the different aspects of you: physical, intellectual, social, mental, emotional, spiritual. Next, move into the things you love doing and the foods you love the taste of and notice how you are BEing when you are doing and tasting those things. That is the vibration you are to vibrate. Notice where in your body you most feel that vibration. Lock onto it and close your eyes, spread your arms and see that vibration spreading through your entire body. We are getting you familiar with the feelings of the vibration of being love. The goal is to become truly, madly, deeply in love with you. Feel whole and complete within yourself. Then you can step into the loving relationship you will magnetize, where you both co-create this relationship being love.

BE Alive

The secret of living a life of fulfillment is to come alive knowing that this body is the vessel of fulfillment. How can you come alive at any moment, in any circumstance? Notice what is around you that is brimming with aliveness in this moment. Connect to all that is alive and vibrant, to all that makes you smile and embrace life. As you connect more and more and more with it, you will start to step into your own calling. Notice how you are being when this occurs. The first step is to be in this vibration and to dance the Alive Now dance by swinging with the rhythms of all that is right there in front of you. The key to aliveness is presence; it is about being present in the moment, moment by moment.

PART FOUR:

TO BE LIST OR TO DO LIST

This part covers the birth of the BE. I share it as it occurred. Even I was surprised at the visions and the messages that arrived, how detailed and profound they were. It was almost like a fairytale, and yet it was happening in real time, unfolding within me. My former self would have dismissed it all as fantasy, yet it was the start of a series of experiences that opened up entirely new realms inside of me. I invite you to just come along with me on this journey and simply receive its transformative and beneficial wisdom as I did. Ask yourself how this could benefit you in addressing the situations that you are dealing with in your own life.

Once I received the gift of the BE, I applied it and analyzed my application of it in a logical way. Feel free to use it to have your own experience of transformation on tap.

CHAPTER 12:

Sounds of Heaven

Clearing the Debris

I returned to Bali after the wedding. It looked like I had just had a facelift: tight, baby-soft skin with some dark pigmentation patches. I booked myself in for a colonic cleanse soon after I returned. My colon hydrotherapist thought I wanted a clean-up after heavy foods at the Indian wedding. I just allowed her to do what she did best. I began releasing almost from the minute we started. Her approach to a colon cleanse is gentle and effective. She has designed her own machines that are manufactured for her in Europe. She is especially good at deep extractions of stubborn, impacted matter, so I felt I could trust her to release whatever was left over of mama parasite.

Within a few minutes, she was staring intently at the tubes carrying stuff out of my colon. Her jaw dropped and her eyes widened as she exclaimed, "What is *this*? Oh my gosh, oh my gosh, it looks like a carcass of some kind, something you have been carrying within you. It's going on and on and ON! I am so happy you are doing this today, you could be poisoned by its toxic release into your bloodstream. Whatever you did in India was just perfect. These large ones can stay within people forever. I wonder if we will see its head today..." She could not stop talking. I finally told her what I had done and she was grateful to have played her part in clearing my system.

After the session, I had an instant boost of energy. The taste in my mouth had changed, too; a sweetness returned, and I knew that I had done the right thing. On the third and final day of my colonic cleanse, we released two heads. Two years later I did another deep cleanse and had practically no parasites.

I know now that the work that was performed so diligently and lovingly by Archangel Michael and my metaphysical team did remove the lower forms of energy and dark forces from within me as well as from my field.

At that point I was ready to do what I usually do when I return to Bali after a break: to enter my spiritual chamber and stay there for a day and half, to meditate, release, receive and evolve. My beautiful housekeeper and cook gave the gifts of their services with a smile. I was well nourished with green juice, aloe vera, coconut and vanilla juice, jamu (an Indonesian herbal drink made with turmeric), and papaya, moringa and chia seed smoothies. I also drank lots and lots of Kangen water. I asked to be shown the vision for the next stage of my journey, and opened myself to receive anything else that my metaphysical family and team might wish to bring. I had counseling sessions with my guides and acted on what they shared with me. I felt like I was in heaven, in the land of the gods, in the tropical paradise Bali.

BE Lesson with Indra (the Lord of Heaven)

I entered my meditation with a big beaming smile on my face. I dove right in and went deep, deeper than usual. I was filling my heart with love, kindness and compassion and I became totally still, in the complete silence of that special zone, the one that meditators seek. I was floating in bliss when I heard the soft, melodious plucking of what sounded like a harp; then other instrumental sounds joined in. Initially I could not decipher what the sounds were, or where they were coming from; all I felt was that I was floating into a huge white chamber filled with light and flowing fabrics with gold trim. Dancers arrived, bowed in front of me and kept going. I floated forward to the front of a divine room. In the middle of the room was a decorated white elephant, being groomed by its caretakers. I smelled a beautiful fragrance.

Then he appeared: a handsome, youthful being with long flowing hair. He beckoned for me to sit next to him. I felt privileged and sat down. I felt as if he was looking into my eyes and he saw me, honored my presence and thanked me for visiting. He explained that we were in Svarnalok (heaven), and he was there with me to give me the key to creating heaven on earth. Just as he said this, the music rose and the celestial Apsaras did their dance of trance. We both watched in silence, until the dancers departed. Indra put his hand forward, and I put my palms in it.

He explained, *"Life is meant to be easy. All the support and the cues have been provided for humans to use, as they fulfill their souls' journeys here. Rather than using these to make their life easy, they get busy doing, doing and then doing some more. They become disconnected from the beauty and perfection of all that is and start running after that which is not. They focus on ways to prolong life instead of ways to live fully and to come alive. The mind was created as a support system and it is in the driving seat. Heaven became something you aspired to after you stopped breathing."*

He continued, *"Heaven and hell are on this earth and the soul's journey on this planet continues over and over again from one lifetime to another until all your questions are answered and you are at one with your being. That is the God you have been seeking and waiting for. You want to know the key to creating heaven on earth? It is to step in and just BE. Create a BE List rather than a To DO list.*

"Choose your BE Word for the day and then do whatever you are required to do; you will be coming from the choice of BEing that you have selected for the day. Don't assume that the BE Word has the same meaning as it does in your English dictionary. Create your own meaning; what does this word mean for you? That is how you are to be today.

"You have mastered the activity of BE-DO-HAVE, now it's time to drop the DO, just BE and you HAVE. For the next seven days I will give you the A-list of the BE list. You are to create your own meaning for each word and then just BE that for the day. Share your experience with your tribe and then share some more. Bit by bit you will spread this happy virus across the planet, which will fill with smiles galore, people sharing, loving and collaborating in their truth by embracing their BE Word for the day. Go forth and multiply. Create the BE Dictionary and spread your arms wide, expand your wings, take off and fly."

Our hands filled up with sparkling holographic rainbow clouds; the Apsaras returned and sprinkled their celestial dust of bliss and joy into the palms of my open hands. From the orchestra, a soft gentle bell started ringing, along with a powerful, heart-opening medley of sounds and drums. Sweet high-pitched singing drew me out of my meditation and I was AWAKE. **I had the key to heaven on earth, how amazing is that?! The BE Word, the BE List, the BE Dictionary... and just BE.**

A BE SEEs

"I have the key; now what?" I asked myself. *"Well, let's get to implementation."* I was having a gathering of friends that evening, so I decided to share this concept of creating a BE List rather than a To DO list with them.

This was the first time my friends were meeting me after the wedding, so of course the first reaction was all about my face. "Did you really go to the wedding? Looks like you've returned from plastic surgery!" one joked. They had all seen my Facebook posts chronicling the preparations, the festivities and the wedding as it progressed. I mentioned that I wondered what this face attack was trying to show me. It was such an intense experience that I felt there was more for me to get from it.

Another friend said, "Well, I believe it is a part of what you have dedicated your life to."

"How can that be? My life is all about expecting and accepting miracles and having that be the norm," I replied.

"Exactly, this is what the face attack is an experience of," she said.

I looked puzzled. A frown crossed my forehead.

"How do you define a miracle?" she asked.

"Something surprising and unexpected happens," I replied.

"Were you expecting the face attack? Were you surprised it happened?" she asked.

It took a moment. "OMG. I get it; it *was* a miracle, by my definition of a miracle!"

This is what Lord Indra meant when he said to define the meaning of the BE Word and then just BE it.

My first task was to define miracle. I decided to spend the day looking at and seeing all that I was in the presence of in each moment. I went on my own journey of discovery that day, to find out what happens to me when I experience something and it feels like it's a miracle. For example, a big blue bird was perching itself just outside my window and singing the sweetest song; it was a bird I had never seen before. Then there was this thing that I thought was a bumblebee, but turned out to be a tiny brown bird with rainbow-colored under-feathers and like a humming bird it sucked the nectar with its long beak from the frangipani flowers in our yard. Then there was a king cobra, a long slippery sliding snake that stopped and coiled up. It raised its hood, stretching it majestically, stayed still then started to sway in clockwise circles to the singing of the blue bird. Or the team of ducks being herded by white herons; they went from rice terrace to rice terrace, quacking away, pooping, plowing the mushy rice fields with their feet and beaks, fertilizing them along the way. Or Buana's old mother taking scraps of bark and turning them into beautiful baskets for offerings at the temple.

These were only some of the many miracles that decided to show up on my journey of discovery and by 5:00 pm that evening I knew what a miracle was for me. **A miracle is when something beautiful happens that makes my heart sing. This is my definition of a miracle.**

So...

This is your opportunity to shift from a goal-based way of living to an intention-based lifestyle.

Create the intention for any part of your life. Establish what it takes to get there so you have the key milestones and results that will enable you to know you are on track and making progress in the right direction. In your daily plan, choose the results you wish to achieve. Then shift from having a To DO list to having a To BE List.

How are you going to BE in achieving these results? You will find that actions will unfold based on the requests and promises you make, coming from your choice of the BE Word.

Unusual openings will emerge and collaborators will step forward as long as you BE open to allowing and receiving support to get the jobs done.

Based on my experience, you will achieve the results you intended far faster and with greater ease than you imagined possible.

CHAPTER 13:

THE A-LIST OF THE BE LIST

I entered the seven-day period during which Indra had offered to give me the A-list of the BE List. There was to be a fresh new BE Word for the day. I was to give the word the meaning I chose, and then BE it. I meditated each morning to make the connection and to receive my BE word. I then chose my meaning for it (**What**), created a practice for it (**How**), observed what unfolded (**Effect**) and reflected on each day's results (**Conclusion**). Here's what occurred.

DAY 1:   The word *du jour:* BE **Miraculous**

What: For me, a miracle is when something beautiful happens that makes my heart sing.

How: I chose to be present in the moment and, as I was carrying on with my work and chores, I took the time to observe all that I was in the presence of that made my heart sing. It started off slowly and then, as the day progressed, I noticed that there were more and more amazing occurrences that made my heart sing.

Effect: All that I wanted to accomplish that day was completed by 6:00 pm and we had the evening to go out and enjoy even more miracles. What's more, I had a serene, happy smile on my face throughout the day. It felt like the day was longer than usual and filled with richness

Conclusion: I realized that if we care to observe and be present during each moment, there is so much surrounding us that just takes our breath away. There is an endlessness and limitlessness to the surprises that show up. All we have to do is to allow ourselves to receive without judgment, to be in awe and to be in the presence of the joy that is gifted to us.

DAY 2:   The word *du jour:* BE **Magical**

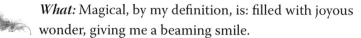

What: Magical, by my definition, is: filled with joyous wonder, giving me a beaming smile.

How: I turned up my "wonder alert" antenna and went about my day normally, stopping to notice where I was and what I was doing when I felt the corners of my mouth turning themselves up into a beaming smile. Just like on Day 1, it began slowly. Then, within a couple of hours, I found myself beaming a smile out almost every hour. By the end of the day, that beaming smile was happening *several* times an hour.

Effect: I became a rapid problem-solver. My creativity quotient went up dramatically and, as a consequence, fulfillment was everywhere. It happened to be a day when we had a number of problematic issues to deal with; in the past, I would have deferred several of these until later. This time, BEing Magical, I found that the problems almost found their own solutions and I only had to do my part, which was a tiny fraction of the effort I would have applied to deal with them in the past.

Conclusion: I realized that when I choose to live my life being present to the magic, I come alive. My experiences are filled with so much wonder that it makes me youthful, arouses a childlike curiosity and unleashes the genius within me. So, when I am being magical, problems get solved like magic. Obstacles disappear as I rise into my full magnificence.

DAY 3: The word *du jour:* BE **Abundant**

> *What:* Abundant means feeling enriched and in flow, circulating, receiving and accepting my gifts.

> *How:* I added a simple visualization process to my morning meditation where I visualized myself owning *all* of my gifts. I saw myself walking through doors and hallways, meeting people with my gifts, sharing them widely, enriching their lives and receiving the same degree of enrichment for myself. This visualization brought the awareness of this way of operating to the forefront and I went about my day doing exactly that, meeting others with my gifts and sharing them freely.

> *Effect:* The effect was like a chain reaction: the more I shared my gifts, supporting the people with whom I was interacting, the more gifts I received. I found myself saying, "Thank you, thank you, thank you," all day long. The more grateful I became, the more came my way to make me even more grateful. There was an exquisite juiciness of collaboration and cooperation, even between the most unlikely people. Abundance is such a great way to get the job done!

> *Conclusion:* BEing Abundant connected me with the limitlessness of the Universe: its resources, its capacity and capability, and its unwavering resolve to be in service to us, each one of us, in fulfilling whatever it is that we set out to achieve. We live in a rich, massive world where our reach is vast and our connections are deep. All we have to do is to tap into these unseen gifts we have been given (they are ours, as a thank-you for taking birth in this human form). Sharing our gifts has a multiplier effect: the more we share, the more explosive and abundant the growth is. All we have to do is to receive and accept, and then just share some more. It's an upward cycle of infinite growth.

DAY 4: The word *du jour:* BE **Trust**

 What: My definition of trust is feeling ease and joy, unconditionally accepting all that is.

 How: This was a tough one for me, and it took the longest to get started. The inertia I had to overcome here was quite strong. I finally stopped trying to rationalize or justify *why* I had to unconditionally accept all that is, and just made my choice to do so. That was the starting point, and ease and joy were the consequence.

 Effect: The day unfolded beautifully and I found myself feeling a sense of pride in having conquered the fear of being judged. Former "foes" became companions in finding solutions and this coming together seemed quite natural. A laser-beam focus was easy to achieve once I unconditionally accepted what is and did not engage in unnecessary dialogue or gossip about anything. This also meant that I accomplished results together with others far faster than we would have done trying to make progress alone or with reluctant participants. All reluctance or hesitation disappeared and we just got on with whatever needed to be done.

 Conclusion: In BEing Trust, an openness is created in us and around us, so that people shed their cloaks of doubt before they even step into our field. This is a key accelerator for getting results accomplished with ease and joy. With no justification required, far more is achieved and greater joy is experienced by all, as we join in to celebrate our job well done, together.

DAY 5: The word *du jour:* BE **Beauty**

 What: Beauty, for me, is feeling illuminated in the brightness of my own light.

 How: In my morning meditation I added a process to bring in the cosmic white light from the top of my crown and allow it to flow into me. I started with my face and neck and worked all the way down to my toes. Then I just chose the part of me that felt the brightest, shining that light of beauty and spreading its beams across my entire being. As I noticed the warmth of my inner light spreading across my body, I went on a rampage of appreciation, journaling all the aspects and facets of me that I found utterly beautiful.

The Effect: My presence became profound as I entered a room; it was like a big beam of happy light walked in. (At least that's what I was told!) People whom I had never met before approached me, saying they had to come to see me to find out what I was doing to show up so full of vitality. Close friends asked whether I had done something different, used make-up or changed my hairstyle. I also felt that I was embodying a lightness of being that I had not sensed within myself before. I felt like I could wear anything, any color, strong or light, and I would look and feel beautiful.

Conclusion: I understood that being in the vibration of beauty made me beautiful, *and* attracted more of what enhanced this beauty. That in turn became a magnet for the beauty around me, so I was walking around not just in my own beauty, I was also accumulating the energy signatures of all that was around me that also had the vibration of beauty. I got it that in my truth I am beauty, and that all beauty around me is simply a reflection of this. I have beauty on tap; and the closer I am to my truth, the more beautiful I feel. I share the gift of this beauty, so that people in my presence begin connecting with their own inner beauty. It becomes an infectious lightfest, illuminating the environments into which I choose to walk; hence the compelling desire of people wanting to acknowledge the beauty within themselves by complimenting me. They were in fact complimenting themselves. I just smiled wholeheartedly, which spread the beauty even further and faster.

DAY 6: The word *du jour:* BE **Grace**

 What: Grace, from my perspective, is a harmony of elegance, gratitude and peace.

 How: I created a practice where every action I took would cause a reaction of gratitude and peace within me. I chose to divide my day into five parts, and at the end of each part I considered all that had transpired within it that I could be grateful for. As I brought this feeling of gratitude into my frontal awareness, I was immersed in peace. As peace started to become the experience of the day, my posture shifted and I found myself walking in the elegance of my own rhythms.

 The Effect: The weight of the world lifted off of me and I recalibrated into the lightness of being that I had experienced the day before. Elegance was a natural consequence. As I chose areas in my life where there had been incongruence and took the stance of elegance with regard to them, I automatically became grateful and peace was the result. By the end of the day I was in a complete harmony of elegance, gratitude and peace in all facets and aspects of my life, including the work I was then focusing on.

 Conclusion: Gratitude is the key to peace. By adopting the *stance of elegance* I created an association to a physical posture that triggered the gratitude response, and all that I could be grateful for began to flow into my awareness. The more grateful I became, the more at peace I was and the more comfortable my gait and presence. All that was required was for me to just focus on the BE, and harmonizing occurred naturally. All that did not serve or could have been an obstacle simply shrunk into insignificance and I was able to just glide across it with elegance, being a magnet for gratitude, exuding peace.

DAY 7: The word *du jour:* BE **Love**

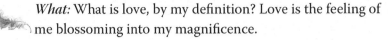

What: What is love, by my definition? Love is the feeling of me blossoming into my magnificence.

How: I visualized myself stepping into my majestic shoes and saw my physical being blooming, all the way into the full grandeur of my full self. By looking and feeling magnificent, I created a number of associations. I chose the color purple as my color; this color immediately puts me into my space of magnificence. I chose the singing of a big bluebird as my sound of love, and the peacock dance (at which I had been masterful at as a young girl), as my dance of love. I declared to myself that love is who I am. I also journaled all the feelings and experiences I had had when I was truly, madly, deeply in love, and noticed these same feelings arising in me as I chose to BE Love in the moment.

Effect: I was inspired to use another practice that supported me to further crystallize the effect of being love.

a. *I looked far into the horizon and spread my arms wide.*

b. *I drew a circle from the horizon all around me, so that I was in the center of this circle.*

c. *I drew another circle from the horizon going all the way above and below me, so that I was now standing in the center of a sphere.*

d. *This sphere became my sphere of connections, and my support network. All the beings in this sphere were connected to me and were supporting me. I felt and accepted these connections.*

e. *They gave me back what I gave out to them. So if I gave anger, I got anger back, multiplied a gazillion-fold, just because of the number of beings in my sphere of connections.*

f. *I chose to BE Love, and to embody and embrace the feeling of being truly, madly, deeply in love with me. With this feeling in every cell of my being, I blew a kiss into this sphere of connections.*

g. *Within nanoseconds I started receiving kisses back, each of them laden with love. I felt tingly, my heart opened up and a humongous smile adorned my face.*

Conclusion: I got that I am love, I was love and I always will be love. I am fully supported, far beyond what I could ever have put into place myself. My support network has been touched by my love and is reflecting that love back to me. I just tap into this never-ending well of love whenever I want to, and I will have it multiplied several times over. I also came to understand that loneliness is a disease of the mind; in reality, I am never alone. With what I had just uncovered I was connected to a never-ending network of loving beings that reflected to me what I was putting out to them, and more. I saw that whatever I give, I get back multiplied.

So...

*Whatever you say to another you say to yourself. So
pause before blurting out anything hurtful or unpleasant
and ask yourself: What do I want to say to myself?
What would love say? Then choose your words.*

*By doing the sphere of connection exercise you will magnify
the effect of all that you put out there; it is reflected back
to you many times over, from the humans to whom you
relate directly, as well as from other living beings.*

*When you are out of alignment with love you
can get into a train-wreck situation very quickly.
Fortunately, it is easy to recalibrate back to it.*

Create your own seven-day plan and you can choose the BE Word of your choice.

Give it a personal meaning and create the intention for the day.

Observe yourself two to five times during the day and notice the effect you have had by adopting a "to BE" before you Do.

I found that doing this for seven days set the foundation of BEing in place for me. I continue to choose my BE Word for the day.

Please feel free to use my words for this seven-day initiation into the BE Lifestyle.

And please share your BE Stories!

You can also choose a situation that is bothering you and apply the BE Solution to it. Choose how you are going to BE in dealing with that situation and then BE it. Notice your choices of words and actions, and then just BE.

PART FIVE:

BE Cause or Be Lost

BE at cause living your purpose or you will be lost

Be cause was meant to be it, the complete sentence: BE Cause. We joined the words together and it became BECAUSE – something we put in front of things to justify or explain our rationale or reason for doing. This quest for having a reason or a justification, especially for our actions, contributes to our becoming lost and disconnected from what we are here to CAUSE.

Let's reclaim the originating intent of this word and **BE** Cause.

CHAPTER 14

BE HAVE OR BE GONE

You choose to BE and you can have, or it will be gone

Gift of the Mountains

The message from Rakeeda, the guardian of the pyramid on Mount Shasta, which came through during one of my periods of silence, gives the essence of what this is about:

Stop talking, keep being and then you have. BE HAVE as you have already learned. BE Love, HAVE love. BE Trust, have trust. BE Romance and you have romance. BEing is the highest leverage; it's where all the resources of the Universe gather together to support the realization of your soul.

Only focus on two things, make your choice for you: be love of self and then just BE Love. You have the love of self and all that comes with it. Your path and journey to fulfilling the mission of your soul in this lifetime is accelerated, time collapses in on itself, deteriorations reverse, vitality returns and you are on a roll. The perfect people, opportunities and circumstances jump onto your bandwagon, you recognize them for what they are and emerge into the magnificent majestic being you are, in full display, being whole and complete. That's the secret. BE HAVE. BE, then HAVE.

We were given the gift of language and the answer lies in the words. We were given BE Have, or whatever it is will be gone. We turned it into a reprimand: Behave or begone, get out of here.

Now that we know what the intention is, let's BE and we Have.

From BE > DO > HAVE it's time to drop the DO. Set the intention, choose the BE word, give it the meaning you desire and then just BE. Actions will flow naturally and you will HAVE the intended result.

Mount Shasta: BE Love, HAVE Love

It was my first evening there. The friend from London with whom I had come was ill, so was unable to leave her hotel room. She asked me to go into town and find another friend of hers in the organic café, and there she was. She shared that there would be a live telecast of a full moon meditation that night, and suggested that we go to the mountain to do the meditation together. I was excited and looking forward to experiencing Mount Shasta for the first time. There had been an unexpected snowstorm a few days earlier, and the mountain already had a base of 17 inches of snow, so the roads on the mountain were closed. We decided to go there anyway, to get as close as possible, and piled on as many layers as we could to keep ourselves warm.

It was 7:35pm on the10th of November, and a full moon night, when four of us arrived on Mount Shasta. It was freezing. We were an international group of women, originating from Japan, Guatemala, Russia and India. We sat on the only bench on the mountain, getting ready to listen to the live telecast of the full moon meditation. One of the women had brought a Tibetan singing bowl with her; we used it as an amplifier with the iPhone when it started to play the telecast.

The mountain was all around us, looking magnificent, covered in snow. The sky was dark, but we knew that the full moon would be rising shortly. We closed our eyes and the meditation started. The lady leading it asked the listeners to visualize themselves as if they were on Mount Shasta. All of us smiled as WE WERE on Mount Shasta.

Once the visualization completed, St. Germain, who is a resident of Mount Shasta, started sending his guided journey to Ascension Day. I was a little taken aback at the change of voice from female to male and I opened my eyes. My friends were in deep stillness.

I looked in front of me and suddenly saw a long purple column. As I was staring at it intently, I was sucked into it, as if into a star-gate. St. Germain lit a purple flame; I felt it in my heart as he was speaking. The flame took over my entire body with a focused presence on the crown and in my third eye. It felt like daylight, except that it was purple.

I felt myself rising, as though I had become at least six inches taller. I felt invoked. Something inside of me just broke open, revealing a deeper part of me I had not seen before. The purple flame started to spread over the ground, the mountain, across the sky and the birds and from it arose a new ME. Everything it touched just lifted up.

Then St. Germain took us on a flight with the eagles and the condors. It was synchronized flying over Canada then the Americas; we were just shining and flooding these countries with the purple flame. For me, the torch was in my heart, shining brightly with this purple light. It was like a scene from a movie: the moment the light touched someone, they rose and their eyes opened, as if waking from a deep trance.

We flew and flew, touching millions, hundreds of millions of people all over America, as well as the trees, the animals, the woods. This purple flame of love was like an uncontrollable avalanche; it took on its own force and surged ahead, like a warm peaceful blanket, a cozy blanket of love. On and on we went until St. Germain stopped and the visualization came to an end.

When we opened our eyes, we were in wonderland. The full moon was on our right, shining brilliantly and surrounded by a blue ring. The snow-covered mountain was lit up by the brightness of the moon and the ground, covered in snow, was alive and alight like sparkling diamonds. The crystal blue light of the moon was being reflected from it and covered the trees all around us.

It was simply amazing. We tried to take pictures, but it was impossible to capture, so we gave up and just enjoyed being there, playing in the snow, in the lap and the profound presence of this sacred mountain. We were experiencing it, absorbing the energy, the joy, the bliss, the peacefulness and excitement of simply being there, then, going through the journey that had just started, the journey of the purple flame.

The Journey of the Purple Flame

I see it, I feel it, I experience it, I savor it, I devour it, sometimes, not all the time, the journey of the purple flame. It's the flame that was hidden deep inside my heart in the back of my eyes, always illuminating my third eye. It was revealed when the veil was lifted by St. Germain, when we were on the mountain.

My body shivered (at first I thought it was cold, but I felt warm). My heart quivered, and my eyes could not stop weeping. It was as if I were being revealed to the world. Bit by bit the layers were being peeled away and my inner light was shining through, as if for the very first time.

The essence of me was here for all to see, feel and experience. And what's more, the spotlight was on it, on the purple flame. I became taller and taller, grander and grander until I was towering even higher than the mountain and deeper than the deepest blue sea.

My being was lit up, though not on fire; illuminated, though not ignited. The light emerging from my heart was spreading far and wide. My arms opened out like wings, my circle of influence and connections was bigger than the circumference of the Earth. I turned toward every being in that circle and blew them a kiss, sparked and charged with my purple flame. This kiss just reverberated back to me a gazillion-fold. That's when I realized that I was now in a sphere that includes the entire Universe and all of the beings in it —not just our Universe, but many universes— and the "me" that is towering over the entire world is all of the beings becoming one. We are united, we are one.

Here is the message from the purple flame:

The Journey of the Purple Flame

*Be one, be the one, see the light, feel your light, be in your
light then take a flight
The journey of the purple flame has begun
It's a land of wonders, it's your land, it stretches far and wide
and circles around*

In the sky, in the sea, over and under the ground

It's yours to enjoy, it's for you to share, keep it flourishing,
do the necessary repairs

It's for no one to own but for all to share

Enjoy it, savor it, experience it, grow in it, grow from it

That's the message from the purple flame

It's flaming hot, it's flaming soft, it's beaming big smiles

It's filling our hearts with all our desires

It's opening our minds to the love we are

Our every cell is love

Love is who we are

It isn't about falling in love or even rising in love

It isn't about loving somebody or even being loved by another

We are love

That is all there is to it

That is the destination, that is the start of our new journey

Just being love

Just being

That's it

You got it?

That's the purple flame within each one of us

That's the revelation you can't hide from anymore

You are love

The one you have been waiting for

Purple Flame

Purple Flame

Love isn't within you or outside of you or around you

Love is you, that's it

That is all there is to it

There is nothing to do, nothing to have, nowhere to go

It's all here and right now
It's in your acceptance of you being love
The journey of the purple flame...
The pilot light was ignited last night
The one that illuminates the purple flame in you
So just look in, feel in, within yourself and find the LOVE that you are
Then just BE, BE LOVE
That's the journey of the purple flame.
Thank you

The purple flame that ignited my heart has remained with me all the way through. We have taken many photos with the purple column and orbs visible in them. The experience opened a quest for me, which has now become my life's mission: to have people be in love with themselves.

My journey to being love and being truly, madly, deeply in love with myself began on Ascension Day and has continued ever since. New experiences and chapters are unfolding to reveal fresh adventures and miracles in my life, as this journey to spread the purple flame continues.

I took it on: **BE Love and I have love, I can BE Loved and BEcome the BEloved, magnetizing my beloved.**

Mount Kailash: BE Truth HAVE freedom

I was visiting my favorite resort in Bali. The sunrise there is spectacular. I walked over to the pebbled beach and sun-gazed for 10 minutes as a sliver of light emerged from the horizon and grew into a soft orange arc, brightened up to become a ball of fire, then spread across the ocean like molten gold. The warm water touched my feet and a school of baby swordfish leapt up in the air in front of me, while a large blue starfish washed up onto the shore.

I was guided to sit down and dive into a deep meditation. Just when I got to the sweet spot in my silence, I beamed up to the top of Mount Kailash, a peak in the Himalayas. I found myself sitting there with my back touching the back of Lord Shiva, the Indian God of Destruction, who lives on the top of this mountain. I could feel the piercing spray of the holy river Ganges gushing out of his crown. Energetically, it was an electrifying experience. I loved meditating back to back with Lord Shiva. I was occasionally brought out of my deep state by the subtle movements of the cobra around his neck.

He showed me that destruction is an essential part of birthing the new. They are two sides of the same coin. He explained that for the new to be birthed, the old (that which does not serve anymore) must be destroyed. Cell memories, which also house the energy signatures of the old, must be washed away and an open clearing be formed, so that the new that is being birthed can be in alignment with our truth, with the freedom to co-create only that which is for our highest good. I saw what that meant for me, and it made me comfortable with this cycle of birth and death coexisting alongside one another. I chose to BE Truth and it gave me the joy of having freedom. It was a powerful lesson from the top of Mount Kailash, a "Beam me up, Scotty!" experience to remember.

Mount Batur: BE Miraculous, HAVE spectacular surprises

One day in Bali, I was inspired to climb Mount Batur, a live volcano. I hired a guide and we left at 1:30 in the morning. It was new moon and pitch dark; the sky was clear and the temperature was just perfect. We arrived at the base of the volcano, which was already 3600 feet above sea level, and began our climb. I was not very fit; I was only doing this climb because my guides had wanted me to, as a gesture of embracing vulnerability and becoming open to miracles, allowing them to flow to me.

So I embraced BE Miraculous and off I went, slowly but surely moving forward, keeping the cadence of a measured and steady pace. We were about three-quarters of the way up the volcano when I was invited by my guides to stop, sit down and meditate exactly as guided.

I asked the trek guides to please stop for meditation. One of them slipped on the lava rock and fell; his eyes and mouth were wide open, as if in shock at my sudden request.

The second guide composed himself and asked, "How did you know?"

"Know what?" I replied.

"This is where they have laid the foundation for a temple," he said.

I smiled, and we all found a place to sit on the ground. While I was meditating, the trek guides would nap for a while. The lava rocks made it difficult to form a clearing; I realized that they must have done some building work here, as there was sufficient flat ground for the three of us to sit. As I sat down, I gazed around me and felt the heavy darkness of the lava fields all around us.

I closed my eyes and began filling my heart with love, kindness and compassion, as I normally do until I arrive in the deep zone of complete stillness. Before I could go in too deep, however, my guides asked me to look up at the sky. I opened my eyes and looked at the sky – it was absolutely filled with stars. As I was staring at it, taking in the fluffy, twisted, sparkly pearls of the Milky Way, it began – a meteor shower! Shooting stars, from all directions, all over the sky, were all around us.

I looked at the ground. It was pitch dark on the earth I was sitting on; meanwhile, up in the sky a breathtaking spectacle of shooting star choreography was taking place. It was so vivid and so present that I could even see the color of some of the nebula in the sky. This lasted for several minutes, though it felt like eternity. Every shooting star made my heart sing, and that singing went on and on until we had a full-blown philharmonic orchestra of meteors. When the theater in the sky stopped, we all stood up and walked to the top of the volcano. The trek guides cooked their eggs in the volcanic steam vents and enjoyed their breakfast while I sliced up a papaya as the sun rose. BEing Miraculous enabled me to have spectacular surprises. I know many people who have climbed Mount Batur and it is only very few who have had the privilege of the meteor shower. I got the message. The key to heaven on earth is BE. It is the BE Key and I HAVE what I desire.

So...

What do you wish to HAVE? The clearer you
are about this, the easier it is to get there.

What are you to BE to be able to have this?

Once chosen, give your meaning to that BE Word and just BE it.

I have found, through my own experiences, that the
seven A-list of the BE List words are often sufficient
to fulfill many desires to which people aspire.

It is all about focusing the way you are being to the intentions you
wish to achieve, and then allowing yourself to go with the flow.

Do be present, aware and connected to what
is being shown to you along the way.

You may also wish to choose stories from your own
life where you fulfilled your desires. Notice what
you were BEing in those instances. That is how you
begin creating your own BE HAVE triggers.

CHAPTER 15:

BElong or Be Low

You BElong, rise and shine or you are below the line, feeling down

Night-Blooming Cereus

I was living in Perth, Australia when I returned home one night and saw a note from a friend stuck on my entry door. In it, she asked me to go down the steps and look for the cactus called Cereus; it only blooms once a year at night and tonight, the note said, might be the night. I walked down the steps, found a pot with a succulent plant in it and guessed that it must be the Cereus. It looked quite plain, except that there was something in the middle of it, like the thick stalk of a flower. The moonlight was strong, so I just kept looking at it for a while. Then it happened. Like those slow-moving blossoming films we often see in time-lapse photography on screen, this was happening right in front of me.

The stalk in the center of the Cereus was elongating and spreading out its different layers, different shapes and different textures, emerging with every layer that bloomed. I was enthralled and felt myself almost become one with the flower. When it had blossomed I just sat on the steps, feeling totally besotted with this beautiful miracle that had unfolded right in front of my eyes. It was food for the soul, nourishment for my intellect and invigoration for my cells. I smiled, laughed and sang, in honor of this amazing display of coming alive. Every moment during this blossoming felt long and oh so rich, and each moment was followed by another, even grander one. The Cereus flower was huge and stood proudly and majestically in its full glory. When the sun rose, it was gone, withered away. Just a one-night wonder — and what a spectacular one at that!

I totally reconnected to the power of being in the NOW: relishing each moment, rejoicing and rejuvenating in it. There are many moments in each second and many seconds in each hour and on and on it goes.

I then went to Manna for breakfast and received this powerful message.

For NOW is the moment of Power

Manna Cafe 2010

Carpe Diem – pluck the day/seize the day, whatever, whenever,
not today.

It's the moment that counts where TRUTH abounds

For NOW is the moment of power.

Seize the moment, rejoice each breath.

Live in the moment, live for the moment, live out each moment.

Feel, think, love, kiss – all in the moment. Try it...

The joys are endless, grace infinite.

It's like Manna – the bread of life, the secret of being alive.

For NOW is the moment of power.

You could have, you may have, you will have, some day, one day,
in the future.

Should be, shouldn't be, can't be, right, wrong, works, doesn't work,
oscillations abound.

Stuck in the mud or floating in the air,

life goes on and on and on and one day – SPLAT, you are dead and gone.

Know your roots and stay rooted.

Feel the feeling, tune into the vibrations all around.

For NOW is the moment of power.

Maybe, JUST MAYBE, you are already dead and gone.
Then it's time to phoenix, rise from the ashes.
See what there is to see, say what there is to say;
write your heart out, dance to the rhythms of your soul.
For NOW is the moment of power.
There is no time to waste, there IS no time.
There is whatever there is. There is only NOW.
Everything else is either a perception or illusion you are running
away from
or running toward.
Stay rooted and feel, feel, feel, feel.
Feel your vision, feel the smells, feel the sounds, feel the senses, feel the
feeling. Feeling is the essence of living in the NOW and NOW is the
moment of power.
You may be powerful and have no power.
There is no power in thinking you should be powerful.
Only NOW, right now, is the moment of power.
It is the same for everyone.
It's real, it's what you make of it.
It's abundant and running away very fast, only to be replaced by a new
NOW. Now is everywhere and always there.
Be present to the now and seize your power.
For NOW is the moment of power.
Thank you, NOW!

BEing in the NOW, in the magic of each moment, you become the moment; your vibrations are of coexistence with nature. You know that you belong and you don't have to hide anymore. You can emerge in the full display of your majestic magnificence.

You feel the power that is within you. You show up in your full regalia and choose in this moment because you *want* to. You become the cause in your matter.

Rainbow Waterfall

A few days later we visited a waterfall, known to be one of the tallest and holiest in Bali. It is called Git Git. We climbed down several kilometers to get to it. It was loud and strong. As we got closer to it, the spray became so strong that we could barely remain standing in it. There was a small shrine just before we got to go under the main waterfall. We braved our way to the shrine and stopped to pray. We raised our arms, looked up into the sky and to the mountaintop from where this water was cascading. As we did, the entire place lit up. The color of the light changed; it filled up with rainbows. There were several big ones adorning the spray of the main waterfall, and with each step we took through the waterfall's mists, a circle of rainbows formed around our feet. The rainbows cascaded through every spray of the water and butterflies came out to play in them.

In the midst of this spectacular display, I received a powerful message that guides us to be at one with nature and keeps us firmly grounded in the now. The connection to nature is such that it confirms that we belong here and that it's time to co-create coexistence:

Co-create Coexistence

Your job is to convince your kind.
You are not threatened by nature, keep that in mind.
You think it's a pest, you keep spraying it to get to the nest.
You destroy the balancers and devastate the ecosystem and
you think you can rest?
Just leave it to nature, it knows what's best.
Co-create coexistence.
You do what you do in the name of protection, yet your actions are confusing
and bear no connection.
You have your values, nature is its reflection.
So if you are bitten, itchy and experience devastation.
Nature is the mirror of your intentions.

You choose to attack it, overpower it, devour it, causing destruction.
It comes back at you as monster pests, natural disasters
causing worldwide annihilation.
Just leave it to nature and it naturally creates balance without destruction.
Commit your kind and leave the rest to nature.
Co-create coexistence.

A message just perfect for these times.

I was in the middle of concentric rainbows forming all around my feet and the powerful spray covering my face when I received this second message. It clarified the concept of Isness, something that my mother had introduced me to at times in my life when I had been distracted and disengaged from my spirituality. This message was a huge catapult into the heart of all that is, that being is the only reality. To be present in Isness is the way of coming alive moment by moment. BEing in Isness we BElong; when we are not in Isness, we swing around like a pendulum. We experience highs and lows and overall it is a rapid downward spiral taking and making us be low.

So here it is. Isness is the business:

Isness is the business, it is the business of NOW

Spread your arms wide, then wrap them
around and squeeze yourself tight.
Notice how wonderful you are, love yourself and embrace your might.
Life is easy, enjoy it. It is your right. This IS yours right NOW.
ISNESS is the business, it is the business of NOW.
What is might, what is plight, what is mind, what is being kind?
What are you thinking about, what are you stressing about?
It is either in the past or in the future.
Makes you lost forever.
The only reality is ISNESS.
ISNESS is the business, it is the business of NOW.
You see color, can you touch color?

You feel thoughts, can you touch thoughts?
You experience energy, can you touch energy?
You can hear music, can you touch music?
You can taste bitterness, can you touch bitterness?
You can smell fragrance, can you touch fragrance?
You sense emotions, can you touch emotions?
They all seem real and ARE THEY? You just keep
going through the motions.
The only reality is what IS.
ISNESS is the business, it is the business of NOW.
Standing under the Git Git waterfall, strong column of sparkling water,
gushing down against the mountain.
It's still, yet strong, it's rooted and moving along.
It hits the rocks, makes them sparkly. The rocks that miss outgrow moss
and become slippery.
It's a glorious display, its beauty in contrasts as the
rugged and delicate play.
The column of water is harsh and rough, it hits
the rocks becomes a delicate spray.
Forming a cascade of rainbows as the leaves on the hanging vines sway.
That's the magic of being in Isness.
ISNESS is the business, it is the business of NOW.
Be in, look in, live in, show in, grow in.
It's always inside out, then outside steps in.
Be still, Belong, get strong and last long.
ISNESS is the business, it is the business of NOW.
ISNESS is priceless, it's for free, you cannot own it.
You enjoy it, it is not the future or the past. It is NOW, the only reality.
ISNESS is the business, it is the business of NOW.
Planning on having it will not bring ISNESS
Remembering your plan will not bring ISNESS
ISNESS is already always there. It just IS.
There is no business in ISNESS. It just IS.
And it is the business of NOW.

I understood that the key to knowing I BELONG is presence, BEing in the moment, connected to and in acceptance of all that is in the moment.

When we are disconnected from what is there right in front of us, we also go further away from what is going on within us. Our mind takes over, thoughts run wild and the heart backs off. Our intuition shuts down, fear and other such emotions begin to disempower us. We go below the radar of our own light and do not feel we BELONG. This is at the root of fears, anxiety and depression. The downward spiral is further propagated when we shut out people, places and ultimately the world. We enter the doorway to our inner hell.

Indra was right: the **key to heaven on earth is to BE, and being in the moment connected and rejoicing is the rejuvenating gift that assures us that we BELONG** and so we rise, connecting with our higher self. We have no requirement to go BELOW, so we do not feel low.

Practicing the Isness lifestyle also showed me what powerful and efficient meaning-making machines we humans are. Something happens and we make it mean good, bad and so on. It is the meaning, then, that drives our experience of the situation. It is not long before the Isness of what occurred is lost and we add another layer to our disconnect armor.

I started to create a list of words, of the meanings we give to a real happening. For example: good, bad, hard, difficult, easy and so on.

Knowing these words has supported me in returning to the reality of what is, every time I get carried away and reactive. I also learned that when we focus on what IS, there is no need to run away from the present, because whatever occurred is what occurred. It is the meaning we give it that makes it catastrophic or euphoric and we get drawn into the trap of reacting to the meaning, as opposed to enjoying or simply experiencing what is.

This is what disconnects us from our companions, our loved ones and from the present. We start living a yo-yo lifestyle, swinging from the past to the future and back again. Isness is the business of being in the NOW, in the moment. I am grateful to my guides for showing me the way and giving me the gift of bringing through these words.

So...

Ask yourself these questions and act accordingly:

What are you present to as an emotion right NOW?

What is around you, right NOW, that inspires you?

Who is with you right NOW and how can you be present to them in each moment?

Where is the nearest place where you can connect to nature including trees, parks, ocean, clouds, animals, mountains? Visualize the most amazing natural beauty and feel its presence in your mind's eye and its nurturing feeling in your heart. BE in that NOW to rejuvenate and reconstruct.

What can you do today to co-create something with nature?

Choose a situation that is causing you some concern, and engage with what it is. Decipher it. Separate the facts from the stories and co-create a solution of Isness, what's real to all. Where do you feel you BElong and where do you feel you go below, into the darkness? Notice what triggers you to go below and what brings the connectedness to belong. Choose.

CHAPTER 16:

BE KIND OR BE BEHIND

BE kind to yourself or be left behind, stuck between the past and future

Amma Hug

I returned to San Francisco after my powerful initiation on Mount Shasta en route to Bali. I met Rianna, my friend and earth angel, who introduced me to the pyramid on the mountain that opened my connection to the Ascended Masters. She asked me to join her to meet an Ascended Master on this Earth, Amma, India's hugging saint. Having grown up in India, with so many people claiming gurudom, I had long been a skeptic. I never followed gurus; in fact, I even had an aversion to them. At this point in my life, though, I had arrived at a place of greater balance. I was able to tune into the true nature of each person, so I did, and knew immediately that Amma was and is a divine beam of pure love. I agreed to go with Rianna to meet her. I thought to myself that if nothing else, I would be in a space of love and connection, just because of the energetic vibrations of the people visiting Amma. I was not going there to be hugged by her, only to be in the space while I continued to download and assimilate the wisdom that had been received within me on the mountain.

We arrived. It was like an Indian mela, a fairground, full of serene smiling faces. I told Rianna to just let me remain in the audience while she did her work. I was going to meditate. Rianna has had the blessing of visiting Amma for many years, so she was not going to allow me to miss out on the exquisite hug from Amma. She knew the value of this hug blessing and she wanted me to have it. She spoke to the volunteers saying that this was my first time there and I had never been hugged by Amma. The volunteers came up to me and asked me to start the queue of hug recipients. So there I was in front of the queue, feeling apprehensive. Rianna had a massive smile on her face. It was warmly comforting to watch her enthusiastic anticipation of what might emerge from Amma hugging me.

Amma arrived. There was a hive of activity, rustling, changing of places, and a vibration of excitement filled the air. By this time there were at least 3000 people in this large hall. The activity stopped, there was electricity in the air and then there was pin-drop silence. Amma connected with the audience. The volunteers ushered me on to the stage, it was time for my Amma hug. I glanced at Rianna, she was very happy with an aura of complete gratitude, I felt good too.

There was an Indian guy standing next to Amma when I got close to her.

She hugged me and it appeared as if she was talking to the Indian guy She was repeating words in English and at the third repetition I got it, she was talking about me!

She said: *No husband, mother gone, one son.* I stepped back, somewhat startled that she knew my circumstance. She pulled me in closer to her and whispered in my ear, for a few minutes. She was speaking in Malayalam, which is her mother tongue. I could not understand this language; I asked my guides to translate her message to me when I meditated the next day. I completed the hug and knew the message she whispered was profound. I felt elevated, ungrounded, my feet were not resting on the ground, or so it felt. There was a funny hollowness in my stomach and I wanted to spend every waking moment in the presence of this Master. In her blessing of me she cleaned out the last bit of sticky blockage from the field of my heart. I was divinely guided by her and totally blessed. I spent the next thirty-six hours with her as she emerged into her incarnation of Kali in the Devi Bhava ritual. In doing so she destroyed the final contingent of demons that might have come in the way of me being on my path.

Here is the message from Amma, a beautiful, deeply feminine blessing that transformed my entire world view and my relationship to myself and my mother. Through it, I became a magnet for gorgeous and desirable relationships in every area of my life. It's a message so simple, yet so profound. Do apply it freely to your own life as you are reading it.

You are your mother

Your own creator.
You give birth to yourself every day,
give yourself the unconditional love you give your child.
Give yourself the best nourishment you can,
give yourself the best in every way.
You are your mother.
The one with the divine wisdom, the infinite understanding,
the one who knows all your needs and desires.
Tap into this and this time, give it all to yourself.
You are your mother.
The apple of your eye,
the most beautiful being you have ever seen.
You always make you proud, even when you reprimand yourself.
You belong, you are loved no matter what.
You bring out the attractiveness of being human.
You look after me, comfort me, inspire me and just never tire of me.
You are your mother.
The divine one, the inspiring one, the assertive one, the loving one,
the funny one.
The one who makes me smile when I am sad.
The one who knows just what will make me feel good.
The one who brings out the best in me.

Just try this one: shift your relationship to yourself and become who you are
to yourself _ your mother, the divine mother.
Showering unconditional love, abundance and prosperity on you for all time to
come.
When you feel low, just go to you.
You are your mother.
Wrap yourself in the comfortable embrace of being with Mom,
the comforting warm soup for your soul.
She is always there for you, no matter what, wherever, whenever you want
her, just call and there she is, inside of you.
You are your mother
Treat yourself like you would your own child.
You birth yourself, what you have become.
You birth your being in every moment.
Treat yourself with the tenderness, admiration, unconditional love and giving,
like you would your newborn child.
Remember that look, that tone of voice, that concern, that joy
when the newborn smiles for no apparent reason.
You give and give and give, with no expectations at all.
The innocence of that baby fills your heart with joy.
Just makes you want to give even more.
You hear every sound it makes.
You respond to even the slightest call for help.
You are there, just because you want to be.
You are grateful for this bundle of pure joy.
Your heart is singing, your mind is still, letting you do your thing.
You are there present, aware, 100%; one hundred percent of the time.
So how about it, then?
You birth your being every moment.
You are that newborn.
You are the mother of this beautiful bundle of joy.
Just be with you.
Be the wonderful mother you are to you.
You ARE your mother.

Thank you Amma, the mother of all mothers for this precious insight. Thank you Mother, thank you Ma.

I read and re-read what I had written, her beautiful message to me, and reconnected with the time when I first became a mother. I connected to my mother and how she had been with me. I looked in the mirror and read each paragraph of this poem again, this time connecting to me as my newborn and feeling that beautiful, soft, warm, fuzzy uncontrollable feeling of love rushing through my being. The relationship between my every cell and me was completely transformed.

I understood that, indeed, I birth myself every day and in every way. I am the creator of my experiences and I am responsible for my own nourishment, nurturing, happiness and wellbeing. I reclaimed my power controls and took complete ownership, resolving to BE Kind to my physical, mental, emotional, spiritual and ethereal states of being.

I continue to be my mother, my best friend and confidante. I embody this beautiful energy in all my interactions, in the absolute thrill, joy and compassionate anticipation of what is to emerge next, from the miracle that I am, which I continue to experience and create every day.

As I transformed my relationship to me, the world around me started to shift in response, as if by magic. I felt whole and complete and the people entering my field started to experience this too.

Buddha's Birthday Gift to Me

I often traveled between Singapore, Jakarta and Bali, on business for The PoEM. Singapore felt too intense to me, and I preferred to get the business done and leave as quickly as I could. I arrived in Singapore early in the morning one May 4th, and was scheduled to return to Bali that evening. My guides asked me to change my tickets and stay in Singapore for three days. Once I made the change, I was guided to go to the Buddha Tooth Relic Temple, where I was to receive a special gift.

It was a beautiful, sixty-two million dollar temple, with rich gold and red brocade incorporated into its architecture. There were throngs of worshippers and several monks in attendance when I arrived. I braved my way through and asked one of the monks for a place where I could meditate in peace and quiet. I expected him to just smile; how could there be a quiet place anywhere in this hive of activity, with the number of people all around us? He did not laugh me off. Instead he smiled and directed me to the fourth floor of the temple, where they had their meditation chamber. The fourth floor was opulent and serenely beautiful, and... completely empty. I found a corner on a raised meditation deck and asked my guides to show me more. I knew what to expect.

I AM to BE AM

I was shown that that day was Buddha's birthday celebration, and his gift to me was my equivalent of his Bodhi tree enlightenment. I had already connected to who I AM, my unique identity and essence. Now it was time for me to BE AM and spread the light of my essence like a holographic beam encapsulating the globe and the field of our galaxy.

Buddha: *Ever wondered about the word BEAM? It is the BE-AMing of your I AM frequency, and now YOU are ready to do that.*

I was guided that to support this process I would receive my mantra and I was to chant this as an invocation of my truth, in every situation BEAMing it so that it supports people in feeling safe being in their truth. I already resonated the originating sound of the Universe OM in the perfect frequency. Now it was time to receive the BEAMing sound of ME, to cover the planet in the yummy blanket of BEing love, where each being steps into being truly, madly in love with all facets of themselves.

I was to receive my mantra, the unique sound of me, resonating in my essence. "How blessed am I?" I thought, as I sat down and began meditating, filling my heart with love, kindness and compassion. At some point deep into my meditation, I experienced a loving, gentle yet volcanic eruption of the energy of love. The lava equivalent of this energy force kept gushing, flowing and covering my whole being, entering my cells, and then it happened, there it was.

I heard me singing my mantra, I was singing it, chanting it, in a sweet voice like a big bluebird. My mantra is "Nityam Aham Brahmasmi" — I am eternal, I am spirit soul, I am eternal spirit soul, I am as God is. First, I was directed to chant it in different ways. Then I was guided to focus on different chakras and chant the mantra to get my chakras to resonate with it. And then I was asked to focus on different organs, to get the resonance of the organs in tune with it. *I am eternal, I am spirit soul, I am the likeness of God. Nityam Aham Brahmasmi.*

I was complete. I opened my eyes; I had been there for over four hours. I felt full in every way. As I stepped out and was walking down the stairs, I heard loud gongs and piercing Tibetan bowls in complete harmony. I had arrived in time for the lighting of the altar, a ritual in which the monks were just then engaged. For me to get from where I was to the temple exit, I had to walk down an aisle with a row of monks on either side, chanting and spreading their blessings along the path. All the other worshippers were in their seats chanting with the gongs and following the lead of the monks. I felt that I was in the middle of a divine Buddhist orchestra, celebrating my coming into this next phase of enlightenment.

Now it was time to BEAM.

I got home that night and in my dream received a beautiful download. This time it was sung to me, by unicorns, elves, dwarves and angels. Here it is. It's time to embrace our I AM frequency and BEAM our light, illuminate our might.

This is the time...

This is the time to speak our truth, to choose, to make our
choices coming from love and sharing.

This is the time to care, to acknowledge each other for our wares.

This is the time to reach within ourselves and find our gifts, open the
wrappings, enjoy them, we have lots to share.

This is the time to spread them around, create a gift exchange and
see joy in people's eyes as they stare.

This is the time to step out of our closets, the ones we built around
ourselves, rip them open and not shed a tear.

This is the time to hop, skip, jump, dance, step up, speak up
and release all fear.

This is the time, this is our time, this is my time, my chance
to shine and create a glare.

This is the time to own my magnificence, my beauty, my strength, my
faults, my wisdom, my knowledge, my skills, my talents and
sit upright on my majestic chair.

This is my time, your time, her time, his time, our time.

This is OUR time, let's spread our wings and take off in the air,

This is our time here, now, every day, every time and everywhere.

THIS IS OUR TIME

PART SIX:

BE LIVE AND BEcome

BE Live, implement and you BEcome
your gifts, living your purpose

This part is all about implementing the BE way of living our lives. As we do so, we come alive. As we embody this aliveness, we connect, receive and accept our purpose. We start living our life with purpose. I share many of the BE Words and their meanings that have served me well to adopt and implement the BE Way.

CHAPTER 17:

HONEY BEs

List of BE Words and Their Meanings

The nectar of BE Words with their meanings as received by me; I tap into this repository often! Please feel free to give your own meaning to these words. The list keeps growing, so please visit our online resources to see a current, up-to-date list of the BE Words to choose from.

You will notice that wherever possible the words are phrased "BE Health" as opposed to "BE Healthy"; "BE Grace" as opposed to "BE Gracious"; or "BE Beauty" as opposed to "BE Beautiful." This is to create the distinction between vibration and action. For example, in my lexicon:

 BE Beauty means *I am in my inner glow, lovingly activating all humanity.* When I embody and embrace BE Beauty, I infuse every cell with the vibe of beauty and being in this vibration makes me beautiful.

 BE Health means *I am beaming, knowing my body heals itself and all is well.* When I embody this vibration, my cells become aligned to being healthy.

 BE Grace means *I am blessed, continually receiving and accepting divine blessings.* Embracing this vibration, I graciously go about activating every action I take that day.

You can use these to get started with living the BE Lifestyle. Every day choose a BE Word for the day. Put it on your phone or computer or wall and embody it in all you are doing throughout the day. Journal the experience or record it at the end of the day. Share it on our BE Blog. Have a BE Sting as a reminder to keep on track and a BE Bling as a reward for yourself. For me, BE Stings are ringtones on my phone, so when it rings I am reminded to stay on track.

BE WORD	MEANING
BE Health	I am beaming, knowing that my body heals itself and all is well
BE Wealth	I am magnetizing an enriching flow of prosperity
BE Joy	My heart is open and I am smiling, a *lot*
BE Live	I feel alive, alert and vital
BE Bliss	I know that all that I require is available to me all the time
BE Peace	I am flowing gracefully with gratitude; there is more and more I can be grateful for, it keeps coming to me
BE Romance	I smile, skip, love, laugh and share happy times everywhere
BE Vibrant	I have an infectious vibe of vitality and success
BE Dynamic	I am alert, active and connected to my bliss
BE Grand	I am limitless, manifesting gifts from infinite, uplifting possibilities
BE Majesty	I am a loving presence of gravitas and grandeur
BE Magnificence	I freely choose all my experiences and energize my life

BE WORD	MEANING
BE Human	I am love, I am loved and I am the beloved magnetizing my beloved
BE Grace	I am blessed ongoingly, receiving and accepting divine blessings
BE Flow	My body, mind and spirit are in complete alignment and harmony
BE Glamour	I glow from within, shining my inner lamp of divine beauty
BE Eternal	I am infinite, expansive and limitless in love and grace
BE Happy	I rejoice in celebrating all that I keep on receiving and giving, feeling balance and in perfect harmony
BE Kind	I am in tune with all beings on our planet and dance in perfect step, making our world a happy place
BE Compassion	I see me and receive my magnificence, and in doing so I see you in your magnificence
BE Beauty	I am in my inner glow, lovingly activating all humanity
BE Light	I am strong and embody the lightness of being
BE Choice	I am unleashed, unstoppable and in complete joy
BE Charm	I am in my divinity, feeling attractive and attracting alignment
BE Now	I am full, whole and complete, enriched and enriching each moment
BE Rest	I am still, safe and serene, embodying my bliss

CHAPTER 18:

BE TOOLS

Vibration Games

Here is a selection of some of the games I use to raise my vibrations to match the BE Word of the day. They are based on the laws of the Universe and I have described them in a numbered list, so that you can understand the rules of the Universe and how to go about playing the game. At the end of each one you will notice a marked shift in your vibrations.

The foundation is that we attract whatever we desire into our lives. This is the law of attraction*. However the precursor to the law of attraction is the law of vibration. When you desire something, the Universe gets into action immediately and delivers your desire to you. You meet your desired outcome when your vibrational frequency matches that of your desire. The key to meeting your desires lies in the vibration games.

Use them freely, as many times a day as you want and most certainly create a practice of several of these that you can do every day.

1. The Alphabet Game

1. Choose the vibration you want to achieve,
   e.g. joy, happiness, abundance, laughter.

2.   Start with the letter A and go all the way to Z and speak
     aloud one word from the alphabet that creates that
     vibration for you.

3.   For example, let's take the vibration of Joy: here's my
     A to Z list: Awesome, Beauty, Charm, Dance, Elephants,
     Frolic, Glow, Happy, Independence, Jolly, Kites, Love,
     Miracles, Naughtiness, Opera, Peacocks, Quick wit,
     Romance, Sai(my son), Tin Tin, Umbria, Violet flame,
     Water, Xmas, Yellow, Zen.

2. Order to the Universe

1.   The Universe is our servant; it is in service to us and is
     at our command. It is waiting to be directed and guided,
     just as a server is.

2.   If we do not give it clear instructions, then it second-guesses
     what we want, based on the questions or confusions in our
     minds, and it delivers what it *thinks* we want.

3.   The Universe does not understand no, not, never, or
     any such negatives. So if we say we do not want to be
     upset, it hears only the "upset" part, that we want to be
     upset, and grants us our spoken wish with lots of
     situations and circumstances that make us upset.

4.   The Universe is only programed to deliver what we want.
     So the clearer we are about what we do want, the easier it
     is for the Universe to act on it.

5.   I use a very simple approach to place my orders with the
     Universe. I draw two columns and on the left-hand side
     I write *I will do* and on the right-hand side *Universe
     will do.*

For example:

I will do	Universe will do
I will BE happy, feel good, BE joy	Give me an abundance of opportunities to feel happy, feel good, feel joy
	Find the perfect business partner aligned to my vision
	Deliver the perfect PA who can support me to grow the business and evolve to my next phase
	Create a waiting list for our resorts and programs

6. The **Universe will do** column has the key components of my TO DO list. My focus remains on BEing at the highest vibration to manifest my desires.

7. I place orders with the Universe every day. I consciously get my mind out of the way and have the order come from my heart so there is no confusion.

3. Rampage of Gratitude

1. Just when I am ready to go to bed, the last thing before I sleep, I close my eyes and make a list of all that is surrounding me that I am grateful for: the pillow, the bed, the coziness of the bed, the fragrance, the ease I feel as I close my eyes, the smile on my face as I anticipate another beautiful night's sleep, the sounds, the sky, the stars, the moon.

2. When I wake up, before I step out of the bed, I do the same. I am grateful for all that is surrounding me that morning: the view from my bed, the warmth of the sunrise, the sound of the waves, the cock-a-doodle-doo-ing of the roosters, the quacking of the ducks, the shapes of the clouds.

3. I imagine myself waking up, embracing and accepting all my gifts and talents. I visualize going about my day sharing these gifts and talents and seeing them multiplied. I express my gratitude for that, too.

4. After my morning exercise and routine, I take a few minutes to meditate and follow this by going on a rampage of gratitude. I write these in a journal and the sentence goes: I am so happy and grateful for/that... I go through everything I can possibly think of that day that I can be grateful for and keep going until I can't think of anything else. I go as far back as I can, and dig deep to find the people, situations, things, opportunities, experiences, expertise I can be grateful for.

5. The key here is to get every cell in my being to be nourished by the vibration of gratitude.

6. I am set for a powerful day ahead, with the vibration of gratitude at the foundation. As a result, throughout the day I attract more and more that I can be grateful for.

4. Rocket of Desire

1. When something that you do not want occurs (contrast), your subconscious becomes completely clear about what it is that you *do* want. It automatically shoots out a rocket of desire to the Universe about what you now want instead.

2. That desire is delivered immediately into the vortex of your energy field. (We are all vibrating energy fields. Given the speed at which the Earth is moving around the sun as well as around its own center, and the sun around the central sun and so on, the only way we can seem still is via the movement in our cells. It's similar to how we seem still while we're flying in an airplane, zooming through space and time at high altitude and high speed.)

3. When a contrasting situation arises, see this as your cue to snap out of the drama or upset. Rather than feeling sorry

that what you do not want just occurred, focus instead on what it is that your subconscious has become clear about. What is the rocket of desire that has just been shot up about what you *do* want?

4. Once you know this, then visualize yourself fulfilling this desire and decipher what your vibration is when this desire is fulfilled.

5. Then go on a rampage of gratitude, writing about everything that you can be grateful for that is consistent with that vibration. List examples from your life in the past, as well those of your friends and others you may know, and write what you are grateful for about them.

6. Keep going until you feel full and fulfilled, and you know your vibration has shifted.

7. Seal this with an A to Z game, listing words that keep you in the vibration

8. Keep doing this for as many days as it takes you to meet your desires.

9. If you feel anxious or frustrated that it is taking longer than expected, then do the positive aspects exercise given below.

5. Positive Aspects

1. If you are feeling challenged, concerned, anxious or upset by a situation, person, experience or relationship, then ask yourself the following question: Given that I am in this situation, what are the positive aspects of this?

2. We are talking positive aspects, *not* positive thinking about the situation.

3. Write them down. To start you off, look at what you are able to do as a result, what lessons you have learned that will prevent this situation from taking place again. What are you able to overcome? What have you released that will free you up in the future? What is possible now that was not available to you in the past?

6. Swallow Your Smile

The smile and swallow your smile approach is used to relieve pain and discomfort in particular parts of the body.

1. If you have pain or discomfort of any kind, it could be physical discomfort or emotional hurt: smile and swallow your smile, then direct it to where you're experiencing the hurt. If it's emotional, then direct the smile to where in your body you feel it.

2. People have shared that when they have a cramp, they smile and swallow their smile, directing it to the area of the cramp; they feel their muscles relax and the cramp release as the smile travels its way to it.

7. Vibe Music and Dance

1. I use music and movement often to lift, shed and shift my vibrations. Create your playlist of uplifting music; your favorite dance compilations to keep you uplifted.

2. I also select forms of dance that help me break out of a logjam situation. For me, Bollywood, drums and the Indian classical dance, Kathak, is a great pattern interrupt. Once my pattern is interrupted, I can keep going and then I am on a roll again.

3. Dance meditations are a powerful tool for me too. Gabrielle Roth's 5 Rhythms is one that gets me into full balance and enables me to feel totally invigorated.

4. Osho's Dynamic Meditation and Gibberish Meditation I find extremely helpful, too.

5. I always like to end my sessions with complete stillness and in silence, filling my heart with love, kindness and compassion for as long as I require.

Meditations

Meditations have played a key role in transforming my overstretched and overstressed lifestyle into one rich in harmony, joy, excitement and fulfillment. I achieve the results I desire, faster and with greater ease than I ever did before. What's more, I also have the time to enjoy and celebrate these achievements. Life feels extraordinary; all aspects of my life coexist with ease, grace and joy.

I have evolved over 321 different meditation practices. I use meditation as a business tool, a personal transformation device, a healing modality and a way to strengthen and enhance my relationships and connections. I am sharing here three key meditations that are the basis for more advanced states of this practice.

If I am dealing with a business challenge, I add an hour to my meditation and often come out with a clearly directed solution, including how to implement it. If I have an emergency deadline that has suddenly showed up, I add time to my meditation and it enables me to fast track or sometimes even collapse time in on itself to achieve the end result. It clarifies and crystallizes the 2% I should focus on to achieve 100% of the result.

I was taught to meditate when I was three years old and we HAD to meditate for 10 minutes with my mom, in our home temple, before we left for school. I often argued with her that it was such a waste of time, sitting quietly not doing anything. She still insisted that we do this. As soon as my little rebellious self could get out of it, I did. I returned to practicing meditation after 43 years, when I started my journey in Bali, and within a few months it had transformed my life so much that I went deeper and deeper into the practice, making it as natural as breathing.

The longest meditation I have done in one stretch was a 12-hour long practice celebrating a friend's birthday. The blessings she received from each one of us after this meditation marathon were deeply moving and profound and a domino effect was set up. She was at a pivot point in her life, seeking to make a life-changing choice. She was the head of a spiritual order and within two months of our 12-hour meditation she had chosen to leave the order and entered the next phase of her life, embracing it fully and building on the gifts of her past while living in the moment.

In giving you the steps to meditate, I have included little practices I have created for myself, to help me quiet my over-busy, talkative mind. These steps have also enabled me to have the blissful experience that is available to any experienced meditator.

I started using any long stretch of activity that I would be engaged in as my meditation. So walking meditation, driving meditation, pranayama meditation, meditation while flying are all regularly used by me to remain connected to my spirit, through my heart, free from the shenanigans of my mind.

Cosmic Light Meditation

1. Sit comfortably in a cool, relaxing place. Keep your back straight; you may rest it against a support if you require.
    I usually rest my back against a wall or the back of a chair.

2. Take 10 deep breaths, noticing your inhale and exhale.
    By the time you get to the 10th breath, close your eyes and your mouth. Let your tongue rest in your mouth, away from the upper palate.

3. Notice the feeling of stillness and relaxation.

4. Imagine that you have a golden cord at the base of your spine and see this cord reaching the core of the Earth.

5. Visualize that this cord is like a vacuum suction pump for the next step of the exercise.

6. Also imagine a thought bucket to the right of you and a sound bucket to the left of you. Both of these buckets are also connected to the core of the Earth.

7. Every time you have thoughts or hear sounds that interfere, just put them in their respective buckets and return your focus to your breathing.

8. Keeping your eyes closed, take your attention to the top of your head and work your way down section by section,

looking for any excess energy build-up, discomfort, aches or pains; simply allow these to be sucked right out of your body by the golden cord at the base of your spine.

9. Feel the tensions being released, and as you work your way down section by section, feel the relaxation spreading itself out as you become clearer and clearer. Cloudiness, confusion and chaos are releasing from your cells.

10. When you feel totally clear, take five deep breaths and shift your focus into your heart.

11. Fill your heart with love, kindness and compassion. Say these three words in your mind. Breathe in love, kindness and compassion; breathe out gratitude and peace.

12. After the fifth breath, imagine a big ball of pearly white light on the top of your crown. It is a powerful light from the cosmos.

13. This ball of light is swirling over your head. Imagine a small gap opening up in the ball, just above your crown.

14. Feel the pearly white light enter your body and spread itself into each cell of your body. As it does this, it is flicking on a switch that activates your access to cosmic wisdom.

15. Work through the different regions of your body and notice the "plugging in" that occurs; say "Thank you" before you move to the next part of your body and then the next and the next.

16. While this is happening, continue to fill your heart with love, kindness and compassion, until your whole body is filled with the cosmic light.

17. Take 10 deep breaths to complete the meditation.

18. Before you open your eyes, take the palms of your hands, hold them together above your head and rub them against each other until they feel warm.

19. Cover your eyes with your warm palms, then open your eyes into them. Next, do an energy sweep, by briskly rubbing your palms down your arms and legs, exhaling as you do so. This is a quick, brisk movement.

Rainbow Light Healing Meditation

This is a meditation I often use if I am experiencing any discomfort, aches or pains, or when any of my organs is suffering from any type of distress. It could be physical, emotional or mental distress. The first 11 steps and the last two steps are the same as the cosmic meditation and I have listed them again for completeness.

1. Sit comfortably in a cool, relaxing place. Keep your back straight; you may rest it against a support if you require. I usually rest my back against a wall or the back of a chair.

2. Take 10 deep breaths, noticing your inhale and exhale. By the time you get to the 10th breath, close your eyes and your mouth. Let your tongue rest in your mouth, away from the upper palate.

3. Notice the feeling of stillness and relaxation.

4. Imagine that you have a golden cord at the base of your spine and see this cord reaching the core of the Earth.

5. Visualize that this cord is like a vacuum suction pump for the next step of the exercise.

6. Also imagine a thought bucket to the right of you and a sound bucket to the left of you. Both of these buckets are also connected to the core of the Earth.

7. Every time you have thoughts or hear sounds that interfere, just put them in their respective buckets and return your focus to your breathing.

8. Keeping your eyes closed, take your attention to the top of your head and work your way down section by section, looking for any excess energy build-up, discomfort, aches or pains; simply allow these to be sucked right out of your body by the golden cord at the base of your spine.

9. Feel the tensions being released, and as you work your way down section by section, feel the relaxation spreading itself out as you become clearer and clearer. Cloudiness, confusion and chaos are releasing from your cells.

10. When you feel totally clear, take five deep breaths and shift your focus into your heart.

11. Fill your heart with love, kindness and compassion. Say these three words in your mind. Breathe in love, kindness and compassion; breathe out gratitude and peace.

12. Now invite the belly of the Earth to send its powerful golden healing light up to you. Visualize the feeling of a warm glow rising up into your body, penetrating your cells. Take five to ten deep breaths visualizing this feeling. In so doing you have activated a healing environment within your body as well as activated all the five elements that make up this planet's environment. It is a powerful chamber that is shielded from any negative forces or influences and you can proceed from there to the specific work on the organ or organs concerned.

13. You are now ready to focus on the specific organ that is causing you discomfort or is hurting. As you move your attention to that organ, begin filling it too with love, kindness and compassion.

14. Inhale love, kindness and compassion into the organ and exhale all that does not serve you. With each inhale, invite the rainbow light energy to follow your breath. It is the energy of love that lasts. You are now starting to flush out of the organ that which does not serve you, while also nourishing it with the beautiful energy of love.

15. After doing this for a short while, ask the organ to show you or give you an insight into the pain/hurt you are experiencing. Ask, "What's there for me to know about this?" or "What's there for me to see from this?" or "What's there for me to understand from this?"

16. Once you receive the answer, ask to receive all that is nourishing for you from the cause of the pain. You may or may not understand, or hear, or feel anything. Relax, and keep going. Just by asking the question, you have activated the connection between the organ, your

subconscious, and your higher self. This communication is taking place, even if you do not feel it directly. In time you will be able to communicate quite fluently. Just allow this process to unfold at its own pace.

17. Take at least five more breaths of the rainbow light love into the organ. As you are breathing, give your cells permission to excrete all that is not in your highest good, and to do so with EASE – this is extremely important. Your cells will follow instructions exactly as you give them and each time you give the instruction, the Universe colludes as well. So, asking your cells to release with ease is important. If you don't do it this way, then when the cells release, you could be in some discomfort during the process. Best to request ease ahead of time.

18. Fill your cells up with the loving rainbow light for the last 10 breaths, and as you come out, it's the same process as before.

19. Before you open your eyes, take the palms of your hands, hold them together above your head and rub them against each other until they feel warm.

20. Cover your eyes with your warm palms, then open your eyes into them. Next, do an energy sweep, by briskly rubbing your palms down your arms and legs, exhaling as you do so. This is a quick, brisk movement.

21. You are now ready to emerge. Drink a glass of water and just be still until you are fully ready.

Listening to Your Heart Meditation

This is a powerful meditation I use often to get answers to issues I am dealing with, or problems I may be in the midst of solving. As before, the first eleven and the last two steps are the same as in the previous meditations.

I recommend that you jot down the concerns, issues and problems for which you are seeking answers before you start this session. You can also use this meditation if you are unable to understand what happened and wish to see clearly what caused a particular incident to occur.

This meditation is a brilliant way to step out of the confusion and hyperactivity of the mind. I have applied this approach in addressing areas in business, my personal relationships, and health — physical, mental, emotional and spiritual. It is the way I distill and see absolutely clearly the 2% I am to focus my personal efforts on in order to achieve a 100% result. I have worked with clients using this approach widely, to the same effect.

Our mind operates from its experiences of the past and concerns about the future, neither of which are real. The past is gone and the future isn't here yet; both are *perceived* realities and are not real. The heart, on the other hand, is in the now. It is certain, clear and rooted in the absolute reality of the moment. It gives us clear, unbiased feedback.

As before, I have repeated steps 1 to 11 for completeness.

1. Sit comfortably in a cool, relaxing place. Keep your back straight; you may rest it against a support if you require. I usually rest my back against a wall or the back of a chair.

2. Take 10 deep breaths, noticing your inhale and exhale. By the time you get to the 10th breath, close your eyes and your mouth. Let your tongue rest in your mouth, away from the upper palate.

3. Notice the feeling of stillness and relaxation.

4. Imagine that you have a golden cord at the base of your spine and see this cord reaching the core of the Earth.

5. Visualize that this cord is like a vacuum suction pump for the next step of the exercise.

6. Also imagine a thought bucket to the right of you and a sound bucket to the left of you. Both of these buckets are also connected to the core of the Earth.

7. Every time you have thoughts or hear sounds that interfere, just put them in their respective buckets and return your focus to your breathing.

8. Keeping your eyes closed, take your attention to the top of your head and work your way down section by section, looking for any excess energy build-up, discomfort, aches or pains; simply allow these to be sucked right out of your body by the golden cord at the base of your spine.

9. Feel the tensions being released, and as you work your way down section by section, feel the relaxation spreading itself out as you become clearer and clearer. Cloudiness, confusion and chaos are releasing from your cells.

10. When you feel totally clear, take five deep breaths and shift your focus into your heart.

11. Fill your heart with love, kindness and compassion. Say these three words in your mind. Breathe in love, kindness and compassion; breathe out gratitude and peace.

12. Repeat this for 10 to 15 breaths, keeping your focus in your heart.

13. Then open your eyes and go through your list. Ask what your heart has to say about each item on your list. What does it want to show you?

14. Jot down each answer without trying to evaluate it.

15. Sometimes your heart will show you colors or visions – write them down, too.

16. If something is not very clear then ask your heart to elaborate.

17. If you do not hear anything from your heart, keep moving down your list, simply trusting that your subconscious is receiving the answers.

18. Repeat this dialogue as often as you require, until you reach the last item on your list.

19. Close your eyes again and take 10 deep breaths grounding out through the cord any excess energy that may have built up during this process.

20. Before you open your eyes, take the palms of your hands, hold them together above your head and rub them against each other until they feel warm.

21. Cover your eyes with your warm palms, then open your eyes into them. Next, do an energy sweep, by briskly rubbing your palms down your arms and legs, exhaling as you do so. This is a quick, brisk movement.

22. You are now ready to emerge. Drink a glass of water and just be still until you are fully ready.

Isness Tools

I have included here a few tools to keep you connected to what is, grounding you while nourishing and nurturing your mind, body and soul. BEing in Isness is the biggest support in allowing us to just BE.

BEing in the Moment

1. Look at what's around you in the moment.

2. Choose each object and observe the beauty in it.

3. Notice the color, texture, sound and all other aspects of it.

4. Feel the joy of even being able to see, sense and appreciate.

5. Smile as you notice the imperfections, and know that perfection is in embracing all imperfections.

6. Turn the volume up and smile even more as you see this perfection and beauty in all that is, right there, right in front of you. Keep going.

Blessing of the Food

A beautiful experience that enhances the nourishing ability of the foods and water we take. It neutralizes any negativity and blesses the food with love and wonder.

1. Bless your food and share in the gratitude at every meal.

2. Give your gratitude to the soil, the bees, the birds, the bugs, the worms and the human beings that toiled on the farms to grow it.

3. BE Grateful for the sky, the clouds, the rain and the sun and the moon that shone on the crop as it was growing.

4. BE Grateful for the rainbows, lightning, thunderstorms and fluffy clouds that accompanied the food as it grew on the farm, and traveled its way to the markets for us.

5. BE Grateful for everyone involved in the preparation of this food and for the people with whom you are sharing this food.

6. BE Grateful to your body; it is prepared to nourish you deeply through this food you are about to eat.

7. Say your prayer if you have one and enjoy the most nourishing, enlivening meal, each time.

* With thanks to the guidance from Abraham,
received and articulated so beautifully by Esther Hicks.

CHAPTER 19:

BE STORIES

The philosophy, approach and practices in this book have been used by people from around the world who have gone through our journeys into miracles over the last four years, as well as by others who have studied and continue to apply this work in their lives. Here I have chosen to share the stories of four people who have applied different facets and aspects of the BE Lifestyle. These people have been chosen specifically, as their life experience illustrates the many different applications of the work covered in this book.

The Blossoming of Cyrus

This is an inspiring journey of a mother and son, Leonie and Cyrus. Leonie was an optimistic, fun-loving mom who lost her joy when her son Cyrus decided to shut himself off from the family and fell into the deep recesses of depression and anxiety. His sadness and sudden outbursts of anger were devastating to watch. She felt hopeless and helpless and did many personal development and transformational programs to cope with the dark hollowness she woke up to every day.

Cy had been a happy, loving child. He abruptly withdrew into his shell at age 11, when he was secretly molested by a relative. This unsavory encounter continued until he was 14, at which point he gathered up enough courage to confide in his mother. She and Cy's dad decided to confront the relative, who basically turned around and blamed Cy for instigating it. A family feud developed and soon got out of hand. Then everyone decided to move past the incident and Cy became more and more depressed. He began taking prescription drugs as well as recreational drugs, to shut out the shame and guilt that plagued him. In the process of his own desperate attempts to cope with the situation, he also shut out his family. If any of them insisted on seeing him, he would go into outbursts of uncontrollable rage. These could occur anywhere, causing severe embarrassment to the parties involved.

Leonie knew what it was about and blamed herself for not having been able to keep Cy safe, deeply regretting the hopelessness in which she found herself, as she could not have a clear and open conversation with Cy. When they met, he would either be quiet and non-responsive or so angry that she could not get a word in. To combat the guilt and regret she experienced on a daily basis, she created a support group for parents of children who were molested and they did some useful work with schools and rescue homes in the area. Cy was on very strong antidepressants and psychiatric medications and that was taking a toll on his kidneys, adding to the worry his parents had about his health. He had given up on education and was unable to hold onto any job.

She came to me when she could not take this feeling of hopelessness anymore, and wanted help in reconnecting with her son Cy. I met Cy and realized that when he was in his truth, he was a happy and adventure-loving 19-year-old. With me, he remained in that space for the entire time that we were together; when he was by himself or with other people, there were only fleeting glimpses of his gifts. I realized that he was an emotionally sensitive child and very, very creative, a genius really, especially in the way he perceived the world. After our conversation, he decided to join the journey into miracles with his mother Leoni.

1. We started by supporting Cy and Leonie to connect with
    their hearts through the Cosmic Light meditation. Cy
    found it difficult to stay still for this. I worked on Cy, using
    the rainbow light healing meditation to transform his inner
    environment into a supportive healing terrain. I found
    many entities, lower forms of energy, attached to his field.
    This can often happen when people become depressed;
    they become magnets for these lower-energy forms to
    attach themselves, which further exacerbates the depression.

2. The next step was to focus on the vibration games, to shift
    and lift their vibrations, getting them aligned with what
    they each truly desired. Leoni started with the Rocket of
    Desire process, understanding what her subconscious had
    released into the Universe about what she truly wanted. We
    identified the vibration she would be in once she received
    her desires fulfilled, began the process of placing the
    orders with the Universe and did a rampage of gratitude.
    Cy was to simply remain on the rampage of gratitude. Due
    to his medication, his attention span was very short. With
    each session, he achieved a dramatic transformation. By
    the time we got to the third evening of the journey, Cy was
    able to spend the entire day at a high vibration.

3. I had to perform the Rainbow Light meditation three times
    during the nine-day journey, to rid him of all the entities.
    Almost as if by magic, he started participating actively.
    I knew we had turned the corner when Cy made a list of
    questions he had for his heart and we did the Listening
    to Your Heart meditation together. He had some surprising
    responses to his questions from the heart. He started
    implementing them immediately. The first smile appeared
    on his face.

4. Now they were both getting ready for the big work, the
    BE Work. We created a BE List that matched what they
    had each said they wanted. Each day they had their BE
    Words. The transformation they underwent each day was

like running a marathon a day. By the fifth day, Cy got it. All he had to do was to BE and he could have whatever he desired. He commandeered our sketchbook and started sketching and then coloring in his creation. We were all amazed at the creative genius in this beautiful being. Leoni could not stop crying. Tears of release, tears of relief and tears of joy.

5. Cy realized that there is only him and that his choices gave him his experience of life. He wanted to claim his own space fully. With medical guidance, he came off his medications and became an intern with a business, where he was offered the opportunity to progress into the job of his dreams.

6. Cy took up art and began expressing himself through acrylics and sculpture. He is now quite often commissioned as an artist. Leonie transformed herself as well, into a smiling woman who embraces a grand sense of adventure. To BE was the choice they each made. Leonie and Cy continue to emerge and evolve in their own lives and in their relationship together.

7. *BE and HAVE* was the key to their reinvention into love.

From Infidelity to Rekindling Romance
Anna and Rajesh

This is the story of Rajesh and Anna. They met during a holiday, became lovers and moved to a new country to start a life together. They were so compatible and committed to each other; it was sweet to watch them set up their new home together and create a social and business life in their new country. The romance and the relationship grew deeper as the years went by. Rajesh was a genius creative entrepreneur, working at being more disciplined and rigorous. He worked from home and on holidays, as his business was online. Anna had a very structured upbringing and liked the security of a stable job and income. They were from different cultures and different parts of the world. Rajesh had done a lot of personal transformation work, while Anna had remained focused working in the corporate world. Both of them were exceptionally good at connecting with people.

After two years of living together, Rajesh had to travel to London for a few weeks. All was well and both of them spent their days working hard and then connected every evening, lovingly reminiscing, expressing their yearnings for each other and sharing the goings on of the day. Rajesh was expanding his network and reach and Anna was missing him, working consistently at making her mark at the corporation where she was working.

One evening she came home from work and the doorbell rang. She asked who it was on the intercom and it turned out to be a surprise visitor, an old flame, an unrequited infatuation interest from the past. He happened to be visiting and had decided to drop by. Anna was happy to see him; there was lots to catch up on, including her relationship with Rajesh. All was going well. They had dinner and a few drinks. Then one thing led to another and they slept together. When they emerged they realized what had occurred and parted ways.

Anna called Rajesh in London and told him what had happened. She was distraught and deeply regretted what had occurred. He was shocked and devastated. Betrayal was his worst nightmare and he was thousands of miles away living this. They kept talking to each other, going round in circles, sharing their upset over and over again. Anna desperately wanted him back and he could not speak with her without being snared again by what had taken place.

Rajesh called me and asked if I would go to Anna and be with her, to give her some love, as he could not be loving to her at the moment. She needed to talk to someone without feeling judged. He felt that if she were unable to do this now she would shut down. He wanted his own space to process what had occurred.

I saw Anna for a few days before Rajesh was to return from London. I chose to BE Accepting and allow Anna to share. I knew from tuning into her that she was genuine, authentic and sincere in her love for Rajesh.

This indiscretion was indeed a one-off and had only strengthened her love for him. Rajesh, however, was in desperate mourning, deeply resenting what had transpired. He was also extremely angry with Anna for betraying him and damaging the sanctity of their relationship. He came home and his anger exploded, as he understood that the act had taken place in their bedroom. He decided to have an indiscretion himself, which only made it worse for them both.

Each of them were still keen to save their relationship but did not know how. They decided to join me on a journey that would transform their lives forever. I warned them that as a result of the journey, they would complete this past experience of their relationship together. As a result, they would be empowered: either to choose to end the relationship or to rekindle their love for one another, wherein a new surge of romance would emerge, with a lasting power they had not experienced or seen before.

Through the guided Journey Into Miracles, they each saw that they had stepped away from love. Rajesh was being angry, Anna was being desperate; he was being confused and she was being regretful. These vibrational frequencies were generating more and more of the same. They were in an out-of-control train, accelerating towards a wreck.

1. The first step was for Anna and Rajesh to BE open and BE allowing, in order to receive guidance and accept the coaching offered.

2. The second was for both of them to understand that they each were, and always will remain, magnificent beings in human disguise. Despite what had taken place, their magnificence was intact; it was only their human disguises that had gotten fractured.

3. The third was for them to practice *unconditional acceptance of all that is.* This was hard for them, but given that they had embraced being open, they did it. I asked them to embrace each other's fractured human disguises, as this would enable each of them to step into their own magnificence.

4. We did the positive aspects exercise looking at this: Given that they were in this situation, what were the positive aspects of being in it?

5. We also did the rocket of desire process and considered the fact that something they both did not want had occurred. What it was that they *did* want would be the order that had been placed with the Universe by their subconscious. So if they actually had what they said they wanted, their desires fulfilled, then what vibrations would they experience? Finally, both Rajesh and Anna did their rampage of gratitude. They created a practice to do this every day, in their own time.

6. All of this prepared them to do the real work of the journey, uncovering the essence of who they are, their unique mastery in relationships, their Source. They each established a practice to BE in their Source and to remain in their mastery every day. They understood that what had transpired was a recurring autopilot pattern that kept both of them unfulfilled in relationships of all sorts. They established their own way of stepping into their Source when they went off track and of supporting each other, too, in a loving way.

7. Now it was time for the BIG prize — to become truly, madly, deeply in love with themselves. I explained that while we are not feeling whole and complete within ourselves, we seek completion in and through another and that is fine, except when a traumatic incident occurs and the blame game sets in. It was now time for them to BE Love, so that they can BE Loved and become the BELOVED. If you can BE your beloved, you become THE beloved. It was time to reinvent their relationship into one in which they became the loving co-creators of their life together, BEing love.

8. Rajesh and Anna embraced this BE and continued to do their morning practices. The deeper they went into their love for themselves, the stronger their love for each other became.

9. Now they co-create and generate their relationship every day. They live a romantic life in their Source doing what they love and loving what they do.

10. An exquisite sense of love and connection exists between them, and they are an inspiration to many of their friends. Both are totally honoring and accepting of one another. They freely express themselves to each other and in the world.

11. At the time of writing this they had just completed a divine soul union ceremony celebrating their love and life together going forward.

From Vitriolic Divorce to Happy Ending
Dave and Veronica

Dave and Veronica were in the midst of a vitriolic divorce. They had had four children together, and two of them had begun displaying behavioral disorders. Counseling sessions would often end in aggression and anger; mistrust and accusations ran rampant between them. Dave felt that Veronica was out to destroy him and damage the children in the process, while Veronica felt that Dave was pathetic and had lost his pizzazz. She considered him a loser who had borrowed money from her parents, lost all their assets and then become ill with cancer. She had no sympathy for him and did not want him around.

Dave felt that Veronica was unfaithful, untrustworthy and selfish; he believed that she did not care for the children or for him and just wanted to get the last remnants of the assets he owned, even though at this point in their life she was earning more than he was. He had been diagnosed with cancer, treated for it and had survived, though his markers were still not entirely in the safe zone. He was at risk from a relapse and had to be watchful. The vitriol in him was so strong that he was starting to look paler and paler, and within himself he knew he was not well.

His energy was so lacking that he was unable to perform as expected at work, so his business partner was also starting to feel dejected. Dave's only inspiration came from his kids, and he worried endlessly as he was becoming less and less able to be the provider he had always envisioned himself being. The lower his energy levels went, the harder he became on himself, and the worse his performance became at work. This reinforced Veronica's belief that he was a loser. She started drinking heavily, partying till late hours of the night, having affairs with much younger men; her attempts at grabbing everything she could lay her hands on intensified. She finally decided to walk out of the family home and life, and to take Dave for all he had, including the kids. She filed for divorce.

Their eldest son, who was an extremely bright child, began flaking out at school; his performance deteriorated rapidly. Dave pleaded with her to let him be the main guardian for the kids, to no avail. She was going to get lawyers to sort this all out. Even her parents could not influence her. She was out of control, out to take revenge and destroy whatever little confidence and certainty Dave had left. He, in turn, became quieter and quieter, focusing on keeping the kids safe and sheltered. The children called him on several occasions when their mother had come home drunk with some young dude. Dave would come at any time, day or night, to care for the children. During the day, Veronica used him as a dumping ground for her own disorganization. She would often call and say she could not collect the children from school. Dave would instantly drop whatever he was doing and go get them.

The children appreciated their dad and could not understand why he was not stronger in his demands with their mother, especially since he knew she was being so irresponsible. Dave maintained that she had not always been like this. Something had happened to her since his recovery from cancer. According to him, during his treatment she was constantly by his side, but when he recovered, she turned on him and became nasty, selfish, uncaring, irresponsible and aggressive. It had become worse and worse, until now she was out of control and he was feeling helpless.

He came to see me in the midst of his divorce, saying that it was shattering his life and damaging his children. We went on a journey together. In this instance I would be working only with Dave to turn the situation around, as Veronica had shut him out and was uninterested in anything he was doing.

1. The first step was for Dave to *unconditionally accept* what is. To arrive at this place we first worked through getting clear on what it was that he wanted. If anything were possible, what would be going on at home when he returned from this journey? I got him to describe this in great detail, focusing on the different parts of his life and all the relationships that were important to him.

2. It was clear that emotionally he was done with his marriage and ready to embark on the next phase of his life. We went through the different emotions he felt about Veronica, and through a process of communicating with love, we transformed each of the negative emotions to its empowering counterpart. He made a list of all that he was ready to put a stop to and burned it at an altar. Then he released it into the ocean.

3. We uncovered his underlying autopilot default pattern and connected him to his unique mastery, his essence, his Source.

4. Now we were ready to place the orders with the Universe using the two-column exercise. He started doing this every day at the journey into miracles.

5. He also adopted the practice of writing a rampage of gratitude every day. By the third day he was a different

Dave, filled with vitality, energized to define his desires clearly and to have what he had defined.

6. We followed the process of creating intentions for the different aspects of his life and adopting the BE Approach to achieving them.

7. He understood and implemented the concept of BE and HAVE as opposed to what he had been doing, which was reprimanding Veronica, demanding that she Behave. He saw that both she and he had been lost in the maze, unable to escape their own patterns.

8. Dave learned to meditate using the rainbow light and put it into practice, working with his body and his vitality. He followed the philosophy of BEing Kind to himself and not being left behind, stuck in the past.

9. He started using the BE List and created a BE Word for each day.

10. When he returned after the journey, the vision he had laid out for what he wanted was exactly what had unfolded at home. Veronica had left home fully, found a beautiful place to live and agreed to divide the time with the kids in a sensible way that supported the children and gave Dave an opportunity to reclaim his position in business.

11. Dave continued his meditation practice and two months after his return he went for his markers check. They were fine. He looked healthier and took up athletics again, regaining his strength and vitality. His children joined him in the different sports he now participated in.

12. At the time of writing this, Dave and Veronica were happily divorced and enjoying co-parenting their children. Dave's business had turned around for the better and was growing healthily; he was contributing his full share to the partnership.

13. The children were happy and enjoying separate times with mother and father.

14. Dave chose to BE Cause in the matter of his life. He became free to choose how he lived it, and came alive in the process.

From Abandonment to Reunion
Nicolas and His Mother

Nicolas, a handsome, blond-haired and blue-eyed young man, was a workaholic, a surfer and a scientist. He had had terrible luck with women. He was good at starting a relationship, but often within a very short time the relationship would feel so stifling to him that he would end it, and then feel upset and low about it all. It would take almost as long as the relationship had lasted for him to recover from the break-up, even though he had been the one to end things in the first place. As a scientist, he had specialist expertise, so he was sought-after and kept himself extremely busy. He worked in oil and gas, so was often sent offshore. His joy was in water sports, which he did a great deal of while he was away at work.

His hair was long, unkempt and covered his eyes. Only occasionally would he push it away from his face so you could see his handsomeness. A smile was difficult to come by; he had worn his frown like women wear makeup, so that even at a very young age he had pronounced frown lines. He felt lost and was desperately seeking some solace.

When he came to me, he shared that he was keen to find his soulmate, and that he hated his work in the oil and gas sector. He felt that it was destroying the oceans and the creatures in it and that these were his love and joy. He said that he needed the money and the distraction from the soullessness of life, so he could not just walk out and leave the job. He was conflicted and confused.

Nic was deeply entangled in "I want to, BUT…"; "I need to…"; "I have to because…"; "I should do…"; "I should not be…" His was a case of a disheartened free spirit in an endless disappointing spin of having to conform. He was living in shackles and did not know how to break free from them. He was desperately seeking to change his life when he met me and chose to come on a journey.

We realized early on in the journey that Nicolas had a secret. His mother had left him and his brother with their father when he was seven years old. Several years later she tried to reconnect with him, but Nicolas was not interested in that. I understood that his mother having left him at the tender age of seven was an unprocessed trauma, still held in his cellular memory and troubling him. He had attempted to shut it out, but at a subconscious level it was still actively sabotaging his relationships with women. They were a representation of that experience. He would leave them before they could leave him, so that he could not feel abandoned. He was always on the edge, neither sharing himself nor vesting himself fully in any relationship. He also had trained himself to hold back, never expressing how he felt or what he wanted, because he did not feel anyone cared or was interested in him.

1.   First thing we did was to reveal to Nic his autopilot default patterning, so he could see how he kept repeating dysfunctional, disengaged relationships.

2.   Next we connected him to the essence of who he truly is, his unique mastery. He connected with his unique capability, which was to have people trust and love themselves for who they truly are. He realized that he had become completely disconnected from loving and trusting himself. He also understood why he loved the ocean and the creatures in it so much; they are this way, in their truth and in complete harmony with themselves and their natural environment. Once he connected with his Source and accepted his own mastery, he experienced waves and waves of tingles for several hours, as his body recalibrated into his truth.

3.   Then we moved to unconditionally accepting all that is. At this point we unveiled that his father had been a violent alcoholic. He was a control freak who had married Nic's mother in Russia and then brought her to live in a faraway land. She had been violently and repeatedly attacked by Nic's father until she could take it no more and left.

4.   Nicolas understood that his mother was as equally magnificent as he was or as his father was. Their human disguises had been fractured. Coming from his Source, he embraced his parents' human disguises as well as his own. Now he was ready to do the real work.

5.   Nic focused on Isness and started his journey to living in the moment. He realized that he BELONGED, and did not need to go below to hide out. During the journey, his lovely blond hair was tied back in a ponytail and when he returned to the mainland he had a haircut after many years. His forehead eased up and the frown lines diminished. He stood up straight and looked at least four inches taller. He chose to go camping with his dad and enjoyed every moment of their trip.

6.   He diligently applied the many vibration games from the BE Tools. The first one he engaged with was the positive aspects exercise, and he answered the question: Given that he is in this situation what are the positive aspects of this? He was shocked, surprised and an emotional wreck when he saw he had filled up more than two solid pages with positive aspects. Nic's vibrations shifted and he became hopeful.

7.   He decided to BE Cause and declared that his life was going to change. He was going to work for only three months a year; he would live in a place by the ocean with his soulmate; and he would meet his mother.

8.   On returning to the mainland from the journey, he decided to meet his mother. It had been 14 years since he

had seen her. Within three months he had found his soulmate and within six months he had restructured his life to work for only three months a year, still earning nearly as much as he did working full time. He and his love moved to live by the ocean in a surfer's paradise.

9.   He brought his mother to meet me, and she could not stop talking about her son. She shared that she originally left because she felt that her sons' lives were in danger if she stayed, as their father's violence was becoming more and more severe. She did not have any family in the country she was in, so to feel safe she returned to Russia, which at the time was behind the Iron Curtain. Due to travel restrictions she could not take her children with her on that trip; when she came back for them a few months later, her husband made it impossible for her to even meet them. When she called to speak with them, the children were being dictated to in the background, so they never spoke with her. Now that they were reunited, she was so proud of her Nicolas and who he had become. She could not stop smiling and was beaming like an angel. She had come to my home to a gathering of friends and became the heart of the party. Nicolas, who in the past would have been a shy wallflower, was now walking around tall and handsome, sharing his vision and excitement for his life going forward and feeling so happy in his heart seeing his mother. He could not stop smiling.

10.   He chose to BE Cause and let himself BEcome the magnificent being he was, in his truth.

11.   At the time of writing this story, Nicolas and his beloved are happily settled and love BEing Love, being loved and being in love, co-creating joy in their life together by the ocean.

12.   The BE Word practice is a way of life for Nicolas, as he continues to grow and flourish.

PART SEVEN:

TO BE OR NOT TO BE...
What is Your Answer?

The biggest gift of the BE is the connection to ME. By that I mean to you, yourself. Keeping yourself in the BE state, you unlock the doorways to infinite possibilities and an endless flow of miracles. You do so easily and effortlessly, enjoying every step of the journey while also nourishing your mind, body and soul.

The BE is a deep embodiment of a simple understanding that there is only YOU, and the entire Universe is in service to you. All your experiences are a reflection of who you are BEing at that moment. It is NOT about what you are doing. The doing focus is the busy-ness distraction that you allowed yourself to become embroiled in; it's an easy and effective way to get yourself all tangled up.

You can, if you so choose, step out of this entanglement with a BE Sting. Choose to BE. In doing so, you rise up and step into your FULL grand magnificence; you become the Superhero for yourself and you can just lift off, leaving behind the debris of shackles and chains that were previously keeping you trapped.

Are you ready to take this flight?
Join us and Make the BE Move.

CHAPTER 20:

MAKING THE BE MOVE

How readers are using the BE Book

The BE Book is specifically designed to be valuable to people going through a transformational moment, a significant transition in their lives. They must make a choice; they are at a pivot point in their life. At one end of that pivot point is fear and at the other end is love. This book is written to support people in making their choice by rising above the fear and coming from love.

With this in mind, when I completed the first draft of this book, I sent it to a selection of people in different states of transition, including: new relationship; recently graduated and embarking on a new career; moving to a new country; Saturn return; recovering from a major health situation; entering a new phase in their life; calling in living their life with purpose; dramatic change in business (positive and negative); breakdown and breakthrough in continuing relationships. I chose men and women in different age brackets from 19 to 72 years of age.

Each gave me their feedback within a few short weeks, and many continue to keep me apprised of how they are using the book. To support you in making the BE Move yourself, I share here fifteen practical ways in which this book is being used and applied by these readers. Please feel free to use these ideas to optimize the value you derive from this work.

1. When you have a question or are looking for external help with something, then use the book like an oracle. Just open the book and read the content of the page(s) you opened to. Distill from that the insights and lessons that you can apply to address your situation.

2. Choose your BE Word for the day. One couple has extracted the list in the *Honey BEs* section in Part 6 and have placed it on their altar. After their morning practices they choose their BE Word for the day.

3. Use the *A-List of the BE List* from Part 4 to create your own seven-day journey of BE transformation. People are using this and noticing the effect and impact they experience every day. The results are quite juicy and amazing.

4. Several readers, who have had difficult times and experiences that they chose to shut out of their active memory, are now embracing what is. They are engaging with the gifts that have become available to them from those incidents. I receive messages about the ways of BEING that were formed during those traumatic times; they are using the lessons arising from them as a way of healing the emotional and physical effects of those traumatic situations. They all report an uplifting sense of freedom that has emerged for them, where they do not have to hide any more, even from themselves. They are rising and expanding into their full magnificence.

5. The message from Amma, "You are your mother..." in Chapter 16 is being used by some readers as a way to start loving themselves, and as a tool of forgiveness, acceptance and self-love.

6. Many new meditators have used the Cosmic Light meditation practice in the BE Tools section and have learned to silence their mind and distractions using the thought and sound buckets.

7.   Experienced meditators have begun using Rainbow Light meditations to self-heal and complete processing unfinished issues.

8.   The Listening to Your Heart meditation is actively used by several readers, particularly when they are overwhelmed by too many choices or opinions. It enables them to see the forest for the trees.

9.   The Rocket of Desire exercise in the BE Tools section is accelerating breakthroughs that people are experiencing from some pretty serious breakdowns in their lives. They've shared with me that every breakdown is now an opportunity for a glorious breakthrough, and so paves the way for them to meet their desires.

10. The alphabet vibration game in the BE Tools, used by so many now, continues to work its magic. People use this game to turn around upsets in their families, with children, before job interviews, to release tension that they may be bringing home from work or vice versa, and to diffuse upsets at work or even with complete strangers.

11. The Blessing of the Food and the Isness processes are connecting people to the magic of all that is before them. Some have said that meal times have become like a divine meditation. Food tastes better (and I predict that it is more nourishing, too!).

12. The BE HAVE philosophy has been applied by some readers to break free from old shackles and confinements. They become clear about their intention, choose how they are to BE, and then BE Certain knowing that they will HAVE what they have set out to achieve. I often hear that business stopped, they started seeing clearly what they had to do next, one thing led to another and voilà, they got what they wanted. BE and HAVE is becoming quite a hero.

13. BE CAUSE has removed the need for justification and excuses. People have this phrase set as a reminder on their screen savers and even have set a bell to ring every hour so that they step into BEING the Cause in all their matters.

14. With this feedback from the readers we have now created the BE Cards. People are using these as a way to set context for how they make choices and decisions. The results are quite astounding.

CHAPTER 21

READERS' FEEDBACK

The book is truly magical. What I got to realize was that there is a crossroad for me, I did this journey, I found my higher self, I know my source, I found my life partner, I came out on top, again and again, but what has been shown to me is that I have a way of being that I need to transform in the way I run my relationships.
This book has given me that.
Thank you, thank you, thank you.

Reading the part about you as a kid reconnected me to myself. It was uncanny. I have never read someone write about themselves so much that it resonated with me on every level. Thank you for connecting me to me as a girl, and reminding me how unique and amazing I was, and how much I used to shock people and enliven them. I was just being connected and completely "unleashed" to the magic of life.
That is all there was. So thank you.

LIJA is currently going through a transformational transition in her life. She has moved to a new country, gotten married and is changing her career path completely. She is a transformation leader herself, a fashion designer and an educator.

*To me a common theme in the book was allowing. Mynoo allows
everything. THERE IS SO MUCH FREEDOM IN THAT! We are
taught to control situations, or fix them, or make it so… but what
would happen if we just totally allow situations or agreements to
conspire? What if there is total trust in the nature of things?
Life is meant to be easy!!*

*I want to say that the backstory and autobiographical component of
this book was pivotal. I say this because we start out with Mynoo as
a child and watch her grow. She becomes very 'human' very fast and
is so relatable in her way that you realize Mynoo is a person, flawed,
full of character, learning, experiencing things, just like the rest of us.
She is relatable and human in this way, so it is almost as if,
if she can be this way, can I also?*

AMANDA, in her early 30s, is slowly coming into her calling by
becoming true to herself. She has struggled to discover the right
path and has used this book to help her experience her journey more
authentically. She is an executive PA for the CEO of a multi-billion
dollar corporation.

*For me, the book was a lifesaver, as I am going through my own
processes of heart opening and sometimes my mind walked me to the
borders of insanity (trying to name the nameless) with no one to turn
to. I am so grateful that you let me read it, it has enabled me to find a
new sense of trust in life and its processes. Thank you.*

*I loved best the practical exercises, like the rampage of gratitude and
the A to Z exercise. It did bring a lot of clarity to my personal path
at this moment in time. I'm so grateful as it really helped me anchor
some core notions into myself and to alleviate lots of the doubts I
was encountering. It helped me create some clear guidelines on how*

to incorporate the BEING experience in my daily life, which I was
having difficulties with. The exercises that I did are clear and simple
and they do deliver instant results.

HINDY, in her 40s, is going through a major spiritual awakening.
It is a wild, multidimensional experience and she has found herself
quite confused at times. She is using this book as a reminder
and guideline to some essential steps on this journey. She is a
multifaceted being, a mother of two, a healer, creator and facilitator
of "the path to clarity" and other mind repatterning techniques.

You described the process of returning to one's authentic, essential self
really well. As you know, this is an archetypal human journey. There
are many ways to make this journey depending on one's spiritual
practice, culture and guides. I think how you described your process
and the way you wrote it has universality so a large number of people
will 'get it' and benefit from it.

I liked the multidimensionality and breadth of BE practices to help
respond to the many different experiences life provides us. The BE
Book is an effective handbook to help you change your views and
patterns in a way that brings forth your essential best self. The book
maps a path to true, wholesome joy.

ADAM, in his 50s, who restructured his life to fully express his
spirituality and gifts. He is a social entrepreneur specializing in the
creation and application of new business models to address large,
intractable global issues.

*I found the stories totally captivating. You are a great storyteller!
I also liked the clever wisdom and all the 'Be' words and concepts.
Overall, it provided a lot more value than most other personal
development or spiritual books.*

*I liked the real detailed narrative of exactly what happened to you as
you went through these experiences and the insights helped me.*

MINDY, in her late 40s, has coached over a thousand published
authors and now runs a small company with over 100 titles. She is
presently re-examining her life and exploring what's next for her.

*Given the life changes that have happened for me in the recent past,
this book was a gift! The overall message for people going through a
life transition comes out very clearly. The messages were so profound
and beautifully worded, the book was full of wonderful wisdom,
applicable possibly to everyone through all phases of life! Yet it
seemed so personal, like every message was written for me.*

*It got me all excited as it really helped me understand how life can be
turned around, no matter the situation. I am often baffled by change
because when things seem beyond my control, they bring me down.
It's so eye-opening to see that everything is internal! If I choose to just
BE happy or BE love - that will be me and that will be my world.*

*The poem of the Journey of the Purple Flame was magical. I had
this warm feeling in my heart while reading it. The imagery is just
stunning! It reminded me of when I was a little girl watching A Whole
New World from Aladdin for the first time, awestruck.*

SAMEERA is in her late 20s. It is her wedding that is featured in
the book, she has watched Mynoo transform first-hand through her
journey and reading the book has given her an understanding of
what actually happened. She is emerging into a new phase in her life,
adjusting to married life, as well as to a new career in a new country.

I've read the book and feel like I am you. Or that I've been with you in your little pocket having experienced what you've experienced. Like your decisions were mine and your rebellious nature was mine. It's brought me to the conclusion that if Mynoo, someone I understand now more than I do myself, can create a life where the Universe presents her with all that she may need in order to simply BE, then so can I! This book has sort of given me a direction. It's taken away a lot of helplessness I was feeling. I now know that I am in fact responsible for whatever happens to me. All I have to do is accept the responsibility and choose to be.

I really enjoyed the details of your own life that led to your revelations. The BE Book not only provides me with the steps but also the realization that I am in fact in charge now. To BE or not to BE was your question and I have chosen my answer. I am to BE ME - and I am going to work with the Universe to provide me with everything I shall require to do so.

SURABHI has just finished with university and is now looking for what to do next in her life and career. Having experienced a big physical transformation in a short timeframe, she is struggling to find comfort and confidence in her being. She was present through Mynoo's spiritual awakening and is seeking guidance for her calling.

Interesting, thought-provoking throughout, even inspiring and calming to me. You experienced much growth in a very short time. I recognized the various spiritual initiations as you described your experiences. The meditations are clear and well presented. I loved them and have already used them. I am a big fan of all the BE tools, my partner and I have started using them and they've already significantly changed us. I really like your transparency and storytelling, wisdom, sincerity and generosity; also, your assertion of maintaining one's vibratory frequency as the key to it all.

MARY is a business leader and pioneer in her field. Now in her 60s, she has recently met her twin flame and has found that her life has turned upside down since then. It has had an effect on all aspects of her life.

*Your writing and the book flows so beautifully, Mynoo. I am surprised
and enthralled by your quality and depth of self-expression and the
grace, ease, contribution that comes through clearly and is shared with
us, your readers, via every word of yours. You have produced a winner
and a major contribution with your book. I am totally moved, touched
and inspired.*

*I've always "gotten" you intuitively. You have always resonated with
me. Yet, I get you even more with this book. I am 1000% proud of you,
especially as I have an idea of what it took to travel through your journey
and to express yourself through the book, your writing. Even knowing
you, your power and empowering ways; what you are about and up
to creating in the world, for individuals, again, you have unexpectedly
surprised me by the beauty, flow, and the difference you can make for
each person reading your BE book. The structure is well done too, again
marvelous. It all works effectively.*

SARA, in her early 50s, is an academic, public policy oriented
political economist, who is currently excitedly discovering she is a
social entrepreneur. She is going through her own journey of self-
actualization after having experienced a series of traumatic incidents
in her personal life and in her career. She is finding her new path and
exploring where in the world she is to operate from.

*Your book is hypnotic, so much I did not know you did, my life
unleashed. I could not put the book down. I was shaking, vibrating as
I was reading it. The language of BE awakened my brain, gave me
a mode of concentration. It is very exciting for me as a beginner.
It is an eye-opener.*

*I loved everything, the best was that I can now meditate. I loved the
meditation samples, the BE list and the BE words. I have it in my
shrine now and after my prayers in the morning
I choose my BE word for the day.*

XAVIER, in his mid 50s, has recently united with the love of his life and changed his career, moved his location and entered his journey into spirituality.

I enjoyed how, once you saw where these decisions no longer served you in your life, you were willing to do the work and transform those places within yourself. I found the story at times funny, at times it elicited pathos, and at times I was caught up in the miracles that you found yourself so often in the midst of. The relating of these miracles was profound and inspiring to me.

I loved it when you told the story of your awakening and also your transcendent experiences on Mt. Shasta and your being taken up and into the mountain and beyond. I also enjoyed finding out more about the "back story" of the PoEM.

GAELYN, recently separated from her husband, is rebuilding her life, career, love and joy in her personal paradise on the planet.

GLOSSARY

	Term	Definition
1	**Download**	Following my spiritual journey in Bali, I began to receive poetry and prose from my guides and to write prolifically. I call these downloads.
2	**Third eye**	Also known as the inner eye, the third eye refers to an invisible eye, one that provides vision that is beyond ordinary sight. It focuses upon the inner realms and spaces of higher consciousness. This third eye is located behind the middle of the forehead, between the brows.
3	**Ascended Masters**	Ascended Masters are spiritually enlightened beings who have experienced lives as ordinary humans, and have undergone a series of spiritual transformations (also known as initiations). They are self-realized beings, now working to serve humanity from dimensions beyond the physical. They do so by raising their vibration to a sustained frequency of light.
4	**Twin Flame**	Twin Flames, sometimes known as Twin Souls, are the two complementary halves of one soul. They are distinct from soul mates. Should Twin Flames meet in the present lifetime, which is rare, it is for the purpose of birthing a project that will be of service to the world. The recognition between such souls is instant and powerful. It is not necessarily a romantic connection, though it can be and often is, should they meet in an earthly lifetime. Twin Flames become instantly one, yet retain their distinct identities and unique attributes, like two sides of one coin. It is rarely an easy relationship, as Twin Flames will undoubtedly challenge each other to the core. Romance can confuse the issue. When they are at a similar stage on their respective evolutionary paths, and if each remains true to the larger purpose they share, Twin Flames are a wellspring of creativity and manifestation.

	Term	Definition
5	**Soul Mate**	A soul mate is a member of our soul family; it is someone with whom we have a deep, unspoken affinity. While each soul has only one Twin Flame, we have many soul mates. The common understanding of soul mate is a partner with whom we can have a romantic, harmonious union of bliss. This is possible; however our soul families are more like our earthly families, so some of our soul mate connections are harmonious, while others are not. Our soul mates most often appear in our lives as beloved relatives, partners, teachers and/or close friends. However they can also be a so-called "chance" meeting or short-term connection, arriving at the perfect time in our life to assist us on our journey back to living in our Source.
6	**Amma - The Hugging Saint**	Born Mata Amritanandamayi and now lovingly called Amma (Mother) by her disciples, this powerful 63-year-old figure is known as the Hugging Saint of India. Revered as one of India's foremost spiritual leaders, the only religious teaching she offers is love. Her *darshan* is hugging, and over the past 30 years she has received and hugged over 40 million people around the world. While Amma does accept the concept of karma - that our past actions have consequences that must be rectified - she asks, "If it is one man's karma to struggle, then is it not our dharma to ease his suffering?" It is with this ideology that Amma embraces the world.
7	**St. Germain**	Ascended Master St. Germain is the champion and steward of human freedom. Though he has long since transcended the physical plane, he has appeared on Earth in human form many times and in many guises. His mission and dedication is to the complete spiritual liberation of humanity. He is a prominent figure in the history of alchemy, and master of the Violet Flame of transformation.

	Term	Definition
8	Lemuria	Lemuria is the name of an ancient civilization that existed prior to and during the time of Atlantis. Their land, also known as Mu, is said to have been located in what is today the Pacific Ocean. The Lemurian civilization was highly advanced intellectually, technologically, culturally and spiritually. While concrete physical evidence of the ancient continent may be difficult to confirm, many people feel a strong connection to Lemuria as soon as they hear of it.
9	Lucknow	Lucknow is the capital city of Uttar Pradesh, a state in northern India. Its unique architecture is influenced by both the Mughal Empire (16th through 18th centuries) and the subsequent British Raj period.
10	Braj Bhasha	Braj Bhasha is a variant dialect of Hindi and Awadhi (a variety of Eastern Hindi). It was one of the main literary languages of north-central India before the switch to Hindustani in the 19th Century. At present, Braj Bhasha is mainly a rural tongue, predominant in the nebulous Braj region centered on Mathura and Agra in Uttar Pradesh and Bharatpur and Dholpur in Rajasthan. It is the predominant language in the central stretch of the Ganges-Yamuna Doab.
11	Mt. Shasta	Mount Shasta is a 14,000-foot high, potentially active volcano, located at the end of the Cascade Range in northern California, in the United States. It is the site of extraordinary lenticular cloud formations, and its snowmelt is the source of the pristine waters of the Shasta River. It is the earthly domain of St. Germain and one of the key energy centers on the planet.
12	Mt. Batur	Mount Batur (Gunung Batur) is an active volcano in the Kintamani region of Bali, Indonesia, situated within two concentric calderas that span eight miles and overlook Lake Batur. The legend of Mt. Batur is that it was placed on Bali by the east Javanese god Hyang Pasupati to secure Bali in its place, and that it was the first place human beings settled on the island. Mt. Batur is also sacred to Dewi Danu, the Goddess of the Lake, provider of water for irrigation of the fields of Bali, in the form of the bubbling natural springs that issue from the lower slopes of the mountain.

	Term	Definition
13	Mt. Kailash	Mount Kailash is a peak in the Kailash Range, which forms part of the Transhimalaya in Tibet. Cosmologies and the origin myths of several religions speak of Kailash as the mythical Mt. Meru, the Axis Mundi, the center and birthplace of the entire world. Sacred to Hindus, Jains and Buddhists alike, Kailash lies near the source of some of the longest rivers in Asia: the Indus River, the Sutlej River, the Brahmaputra River and the Karnali River.
14	Lord Shiva	Lord Shiva (whose name means the Auspicious One) is one of the main deities in Hinduism. He is known as The Destroyer. In his highest expression, Shiva is regarded as limitless, transcendent, unchanging and formless. He also takes on forms both benevolent and fearsome. He appears as the yogi on Mount Kailash, the fierce slayer of demons and the breadwinner for his wife Parvati and children Ganesha and Kartikeya.
15	Lord Indra	The anthropomorphic god, Indra, is the Hindu king of the Lords of Heaven. He is also the deva (lord) of rain and thunderstorms. His weapon of choice is a *vajra*, a thunderbolt.
16	Ajahn Brahm	Ajahn Brahm is a British Theravada Buddhist monk and is the Abbot of the Bodhinyana Monastery in Serpentine, Western Australia.
17	The Rainbow Brotherhood	The Rainbow Brotherhood is a group of beings that presented themselves to me in 2014. Their communication style tends to be extremely direct.
18	Night-Blooming Cereus	One of the strangest plants of the desert, the night-blooming cereus is a member of the cactus family that resembles a dry, dead bush for most of the year. It is rarely noticed in the wild because of its inconspicuousness. But for one midsummer's night each year, its exquisitely scented flower opens as night falls. Then it closes forever with the first rays of the morning sun.

	Term	Definition
19	**The PoEM**	The PoEM is an acronym for The Palace of Extraordinary Miracles. The PoEM vision is to make miracles the norm, and its mission is to transform human relationships (thereby elevating quality of life on the planet). The PoEM project is vast in scope and has multiple facets; Mynoo Maryel is the vehicle and vision keeper for their expression. The PoEM begins with programs and protocols designed to cultivate optimum wellbeing for human beings – physically, emotionally, mentally, socially, spiritually and environmentally.
20	**Bua**	(Aunt) father's sister
21	**Nana**	Maternal grandfather

ABOUT THE AUTHOR

As a high-flying executive and pragmatic serial entrepreneur in Europe, Asia and Australia, Mynoo built eight businesses, produced fifteen feature films for Bollywood and Hollywood and co-founded the renowned Inspired Leaders Network. She became a specialist advisor to key leaders throughout the U.K., as well as to the boards of several Fortune 100 companies. She represented the U.K. in major EU policy development for information and communications technologies, as well as pioneering some game-changing economic regeneration initiatives in London.

In 2010, Mynoo went through a series of spiritual awakenings through which she reconnected with the true mission of her soul. She began to enter periods of silence, during which what she now calls "downloads" — profound wisdom about restoring miracles, childlike wonder and sublime well-being to our lives — were revealed to her. She then undertook for herself what has now become the Journey Into Miracles, actively applied the received wisdom to her own life, became her own "guru" and transformed, almost beyond recognition.

Her journeys, for herself and with others, have been expanding ever since. She is now the visionary founder of The PoEM (The Palace of Extraordinary Miracles), which is a movement and for-benefit organization that focuses on making miracles the norm.

It is Mynoo's great joy to share what she has learned with the world, to inspire people to follow their own deep inner guidance and wisdom, and to understand that, ultimately, they are the "guru" they have long been waiting for.

TESTIMONIALS

*"Thought-provoking, inspiring and calming.
I am a big fan of all the BE tools."*

- Mary Louise Starkey, The First Lady of Service

"The book is hypnotic, the language of BE awakened my brain."

- Xavier Médicin, Investment Strategist

"This book maps a path to true, wholesome joy."

- Adam Pattantyus, Entrepreneur & Business Transformation Leader

"Engaging, enlightening and implementable!"

- Tammy McCrary, Mentor to creative artists
and former manager for singer Chaka Khan

*"Mynoo Maryel is one of those special human beings in life who can not
only create magic, but can teach others to do that as well. Her wisdom,
insights and knowledge are captured in this very wonderful, inspiring and
powerful book. This book is life changing."*

- Marcia Martin, Transformational Thought Leader

www.mynoomaryel.com

NOTES

NOTES

NOTES

NOTES

NOTES

Lightning Source UK Ltd.
Milton Keynes UK
UKOW04f0617260716

279231UK00003B/40/P